WINNING BEFORE TRIAL:

How To Prepare Cases For The

Best Settlement Or Trial Result

WINNING BEFORE TRIAL:

How To Prepare Cases For The Best Settlement Or Trial Result

Robert L. Simmons

Volume One

EXECUTIVE REPORTS CORPORATION
ENGLEWOOD CLIFFS, NEW JERSEY

This publication is designed to provide accurate and authoritative information in regard to the subject matter covered. It is sold with the understanding that the publisher is not engaged in rendering legal, accounting or other professional service. If legal advice or other expert assistance is required, the services of a competent professional person should be sought.

..From a Declaration of Principles jointly adopted by a Committee of the American Bar Association and a Committee of Publishers and Associations.

© Copyright MCMLXXIV
EXECUTIVE REPORTS CORPORATION
Englewood Cliffs, N.J.

Library of Congress Cataloging in Publication Data
Simmons, Robert L   1927–
Winning before trial.
1. Pre-trial procedure–United States. 2. Compromise (Law)–United States. 3. Trial practice–United States.   I. Title.
KF8900.S54   347'.73'72   73-18075
ISBN 0-13-960906-7

To Rick, Jeff, Bob, Tom, and Scott —
May you live to see a world ruled by law.

ABOUT THE AUTHOR

Robert L. Simmons is eminently qualified to write on bargaining, settlement and trial techniques. In this Guide he draws upon his many years as a practicing lawyer (specializing in civil and criminal trial work), 6 years as a general jurisdiction trial judge (Ohio Common Pleas Court), invaluable experience as a former county prosecuting attorney (Ohio), and insurance adjustor.

For the past several years, Judge Simmons has also found the time to teach Practice and Procedure courses at the University of San Diego Law School where he is a Professor of Law. He is a graduate of the National College of Trial Judges and author of the successful ERC Guide "Winning to the Court: How to Argue and Win Non-Jury Cases."

WHAT THIS GUIDE WILL DO FOR YOU

The theme of this Guide is consistently pursued—how to obtain the best and earliest settlements in civil and criminal cases. The thesis of the Guide follows from the theme:—There are certain techniques relating to every pre-trial phase of case handling that promise consistently better, faster, and more frequent settlements. . .and better trial results when negotiation fails. The Guide presents these techniques. It not only tells you what to do, but when and how to do it, in relation to case investigation, evidence gathering, settlement negotiation/plea bargaining, suit strategy, and discovery; it provides repeatedly useful checklists, worksheets, forms, and case illustrations.

This Guide is unique in that it shows how to find all available evidence and put it in a useful form, by means of techniques for effective fact investigation, witness interviewing, and statementizing. Nearly all the "how to" literature for lawyers until this time has concentrated on using the evidence in the courtroom; but it can be far more important to the success of your case that you find and secure the favorable facts and evidence, than that you conduct a trial flawlessly.

The Guide is also uniquely valuable in that it recognizes that more civil and criminal cases are settled out of court than are tried. . .by a ratio of 9 or 10 to 1. How to win the best and earliest settlements is therefore of primary importance to trial lawyers, and is the most important theme in this Guide. All techniques and checklists are addressed to this overriding goal. Specifically, sources of facts are listed and techniques presented for finding favorable facts. Techniques for handling friendly and adverse witnesses, interviewing them, influencing their facts and opinions and taking the most advantageous statements are offered. Checklists of key questions to ask witnesses and factors determining their probable impact in the case are included. Strategy, tactics and techniques for bringing maximum settlement pressure to bear on opponents and inducing the most beneficial settlement agreements are stressed.

Last, but by no means least, this Guide presents a formula that will take much of the guesswork out of determining the settlement value of your case. This formula takes into account each and every variable of a case and translates it into a dollar and cents amount, enabling you to enter the bargaining room with a precise knowledge of what to aim for in settlement benefits.

This Guide reflects my own experience as a prosecuting attorney, trial lawyer, trial judge, and law school professor teaching practice and procedure courses. It also reflects the experience of successful lawyers I have observed over the years and with whom I have consulted.

Each tactic and technique has been tried, tested, and found to succeed. They are of the "bread and butter" variety, always practical and ever looking to the development of a stronger case and a more effective personal deportment. . .for one goal—that a better settlement or verdict will result.

As far as lawyer-advocates are concerned, I can't agree with Emerson when he said, "The reward of a thing well done is to have done it." Indeed. . The best reward is *victory*.

Robert L. Simmons

SUMMARY TABLE OF CONTENTS
for Volumes One and Two follows

⎡ Detailed tables of contents appear ⎤
⎣ on the first page of each chapter. ⎦

Summary Table of Contents-Volume 1

[Detailed tables of contents appear
on the first page of each chapter.]

Summary Table of Contents–Volume 2

> Detailed tables of contents appear on the first page of each chapter.

NORMAN F. WILLIAMS
BARRISTER & SOLICITOR
42 JAMES STREET SOUTH
HAMILTON, ONTARIO
L8P 2Y4

I

The Client Interview... Taking The First Step Toward Victory

TABLE OF CONTENTS

I

The Client Interview...Taking The First Step Toward Victory

"The pursuit of truth is always worthwhile,
especially if you catch up with it."
Louis Anderson

INTRODUCTION TO PART I: WINNING INTERVIEW TECHNIQUES

How Chapters 1, 2, And 3 Will Help You Get The Most From Your Interviews

Very few lawyers consistently aim for and attain all the goals they *can* achieve in an interview—or the techniques for achieving them. These chapters supply both. Since certain goals (objectives) and correlative techniques differ according as the witness is a client, adverse party, friendly, unfriendly or disinterested, they are discussed in separate sections corresponding to the witness label.

Use these chapters as they are intended and you will refer to them often. Turn to the proper section before your next interview and each time thereafter. Like sharpening your axe before felling a tree, it will make your task easier and the result surer.

Just as a doctor prepares for surgery, so you should prepare for your interview, knowing in advance all problems you are likely to encounter, what you wish to accomplish, and what techniques will succeed. Ask yourself these four questions and do not start the interview until you know the answers:

1. *What is his relationship to the case?* Is he the client, the adverse party, relative or friend of either of them, neighbor, passenger in either car?

2. *What bias is he likely to have, if any*, because of the answer to question 1, and what response can you expect? Will he be friendly, unfriendly or disinterested?
3. *What are your objectives?* What do you hope to achieve in this interview? Do you want facts helpful to your case and damaging to the opponent's, leads to other witnesses, impeachment, knowledge of opponent's case, or merely a chance to "size-up" an adverse witness and evaluate his effectiveness?
4. *What techniques will be effective* in achieving your objectives in the light of "where the witness stands."

Anticipating The Witness' Bias

The answers to questions 1 and 2 will come easily in most cases. You generally know the witness' name and relationship to the case before seeing him. And from this information his bias can be readily identified and grossly weighed. Is he a relative of your client, a neighbor, a co-worker, a passenger in his car, or a drinking buddy? You may assume he will be a "friendly" witness. Does he stand in the same relationship to the adverse party? You may assume he will be "unfriendly," using the term to mean "biased against."

Does the witness have no apparent connection with either side in the case, no obvious axe to grind? Then you may assume he is disinterested and adjust your interviewing objectives and techniques accordingly.

These are "if—then" rules of thumb; they are by no means infallible. Not all relatives, neighbors, and co-workers like each other any more than all wives love their husbands. But they do so often enough to afford a reliable guide.

INTERVIEWING YOUR CLIENT
HOW TO MAKE THE FIRST STEP TO VICTORY

Of all the interviews a lawyer conducts during preparation and trial, his first interview of each prospective client is by far the most important. The results of these first interviews are the mainspring of his professional career; they often determine whether he takes the case, whether he wins, and how much he earns from it.

It is quite impossible to overstate the importance of an effective client interview. It is the most fertile source of evidentiary facts available to you, but one which, ineptly or superficially handled, will fail to yield its lode. It is the chief basis for employment and fee contract decisions; if this basis is an inadequate one you can often take cases you should avoid, avoid cases you should take, execute the wrong type of fee contract, or undercharge the retainer.

With these possible consequences in mind, conduct each initial client interview to achieve the following five objectives:

FIVE OBJECTIVES YOU MUST ACHIEVE
AT THE CLIENT INTERVIEW

1. *Obtain facts sufficient to decide whether you wish to represent him.* You need not know whether you can win his case nor even if you can solve his problem, but only this: Is there a chance you can help him? Or is he wholly in the wrong? Does his problem require an expertise you lack? Will a conflict of interest exist with another client? Can he pay a reasonable fee or must you take him on as a charity? (See model checklist of questions to ask, later in this chapter.)
2. *Obtain facts sufficient to decide the type of fee contract to execute (hourly or contingent) and the retainer to charge.* Will yours be an offensive or defensive position? Is there a fund to be won? How large is it? What are the odds of winning it? How much time will you probably spend on his case? What is his financial condition? (See model checklist later in this chapter.)
3. *Obtain all the facts known to the client significant to his legal problem, including identities and addresses of the adverse party and fact witnesses, documentary evidence, and likely sources of other relevant evidence.* Use a detailed checklist of questions to be sure all significant facts are elicited. (See model checklists later in this chapter.)
4. *Obtain necessary written authorizations from the client so that documentary reports and records not otherwise available to you may be secured.* (See forms for medical and general records later in this chapter.)
5. *Obtain an unqualified commitment from the client to assist you in the handling of his case and instruct him about what he is to do and not do at the outset.* (See client instructions later in this chapter.)

With the objectives of a client interview in mind, consider the following techniques for achieving them.

THE PRELIMINARY INTERVIEW . . . HOW TO SAVE TIME AND INCREASE INCOME

There is a story about a sixth grader who was having trouble with the word, "banana." "I know how to spell it all right," he said. "I just don't know when to stop."

Many lawyers interviewing a prospective client have the same trouble. They do not know when to stop, even though they have decided, for whatever reason, not to take the client's case. So they conduct a full-blown interview, asking detailed questions and inviting a lengthy narration of past events in every instance.

Their reasons vary. Some of them think it rude to cut a prospect short even if representation is impossible, such as when a professional conflict of interest exists. Some are entrenched in an interviewing habit, never varying the exhaustive format for any reason, however good. Other lawyers have never analyzed their reasons for rejecting a client, so they never prepared a list of questions designed to learn if those reasons exist in a given occasion.

The consequence of this practice of unvaryingly-lengthy first interviews is injustice to yourself, and also to the prospective client on the many occasions when you decline representation. Your time and his time are wasted, and although the prospect may be able to spare the waste, you cannot. Your time is a raw material you can never replace.

MAKING THE FIRST DECISIONS . . . WHETHER TO TAKE THE CASE AND WHAT TO CHARGE

> ACTION RULE: Always determine whether you can (or want to) take the case and, if so, the type of fee to charge, at the outset of the interview. As soon as a decision is made not to take it, end the interview and explain your reasons clearly and adequately.

The importance of establishing and announcing the nature of your fee charge soon after deciding to take the case is twofold. First, if your fee will be charged on an hourly basis, a fair percentage of prospects will refuse to pay it, because they cannot or will not. In either event, you can end the interview and move to other business without much loss of time. If the client cannot pay the fee you quote, you can always decide to reduce it to a manageable level and proceed into the detailed phase of the interview.

The second reason for discussing your fee charge early stems from the ubiquitous fear of exorbitant fees. No conviction is held more firmly by the public than that all lawyers overcharge; that the only variation from this norm is that some charge less excessively than others.

In some instances this fear is justified; in most it is not. Quote a contingent fee or a reasonable hourly fee and retainer and your client's own money fear will vanish. Often his relief will be visible. His manner will be freer, his confidences more open, his cooperation more enthusiastic and the balance of your interview more successful.

HOW TO DETERMINE WHETHER TO TAKE THE CASE AND HOW TO CHARGE

Step 1: Learn the names and addresses of the client, adverse party(ies) and the client's immediate family to determine if a conflict of interest exists. Unless a client consents, you must not take his case if you presently represent any interest adverse to him. Even where he consents or the adverse representation was in the past, it is bad policy to take his case. Should you lose for him, he will always think your loyalties were divided and will almost surely slander you.

Step 2: Obtain a summary of case facts to determine whether, based on what the client tells you, he is likely to have a good claim or defense. How did the accident happen? Where was his car on the road and where was the other car? What specific complaints does she have of her husband that prompts her to want a divorce? What aggression is she guilty of, if any?

Step 3: If the client's case summary discloses a legally bad claim or defense, do not reject his case just yet. Determine whether you can help him apart from litigation. For example, in an accident case the client may have been arrested for a traffic violation. Or perhaps the State is after his license under a financial responsibility law. In a divorce case, you may be able to reconcile the couple and convince the client that reconciliation is what she really wants.

Step 4: If the preliminary discussion discloses a legally bad claim or defense, *and* no way you can significantly help the client, then deal with him candidly. Tell him you can do nothing for him, charge him a consultation fee based on an hourly rate (See Chapter 14 for fee guidelines), and get on with other work.

In the event you cannot determine with assurance from the client's summary of facts whether he has a good claim or defense or whether you can help him otherwise (he may not know enough facts to warrant such decision), take his case. Proceed with your fee determination and discussion.

Step 5: If you decide to take the client's case, determine the type of fee to charge based on the fact summary (i.e., whether it should be a *contingent, hourly* or *flat* fee). Under a contingent fee contract you earn a fee only if you collect a sum of money for the client, in an amount equal to a predetermined percentage of that sum. Under an hourly contract, fees are not dependent on success but are measured by the time you devote to the client's case. The hourly rate is expressed in the contract. The flat fee contract names a lump sum which will be earned on completion of the case.

Step 6: If you select an hourly or flat fee basis, determine the amount of retainer to charge and collect in advance of future work. There is a twofold purpose for retainers. They bind clients to you. An advance fee payment inhibits their frequent impulse to fly to another lawyer at the first dissatisfaction. Also, retainers are the best guarantee that at least a part of your work will be compensated.

Step 7: Explain the type of fee charge you have selected, and the percentage, hourly or flat rate *before proceeding with the detailed interview.* Obtain the client's consent to the fee arrangement and retainer, if any, then prepare a written fee contract and have him sign it.

Step 8: After the fee contract is signed and the retainer (if any) is either paid or early payment arranged for, proceed with the detail interview using an Interview Checklist Form (see pages 109-120).

HOW TO GET ALL THE VITAL FACTS

A client interview checklist should become invaluable to you. You cannot possibly remember all the important questions that should be asked without a reminder. A checklist form geared to each category of case (e.g., auto negligence, divorce, contract, nuisance, criminal defense, etc.) is that reminder. Complete, handy, and easy to prepare, such forms are increasingly used by experienced lawyers. Like experienced actors, they never risk an important performance without a prompter.

ACTION RULE: Prepare a client interview checklist form for each category of case you regularly handle and print a supply adequate to your needs. Use the appropriate form for every initial interview and be certain each question is asked and answered. Then consider what unique facts not covered by the checklist may be helpful in each specific case and add those questions to the list.

How To Use A Checklist For Clarity, Completeness, And Fast Reference

Not only are facts secured in checklist form more comprehensive, they are more comprehensible. Each fact is written with the question it answers and all facts pertaining to a single subject matter are grouped together. Now don't you recognize the typical problems this format resolves? How often have you opened a client's file in search of certain facts, months after his initial interview, and found gibberish? Bits and pieces of apparently unrelated data?

When was the last time you looked in a divorce file seeking facts supporting your grounds? Did you have to read through five pages of notes before finding them? Were the notes indecipherable because you had to write fast? Or did you find the statement; "Struck on the face June 8, 1971," standing alone, without any explanation as to who hit whom, where, for what reason and under what circumstances?

Here are two checklist forms that will help you in your practice. The first pertains to an automobile personal injury or property damage case and the second to a divorce case.

SAMPLE CHECKLIST FORMS

Checklist For Automobile Personal Injury Case—Client Interview

A. Client—Personal

1. Date _____ File # _____
2. Name _____ Address _____
3. Marital Status _____ Age _____ Phone _____
4. Spouse Name _____ Employment _____
5. Employment, past and present _____
   _____

6. Prior Accidents, dates and locations _____

_____

7. Prior Injuries, dates and descriptions _____

_____

8. Arrests and convictions _____
9. Liability insurance _____ Coverage _____
10. Collision insurance _____ Coverage _____
11. Uninsured Motorist Coverage _____ Medical Payment

Coverage _____

B. Adverse Party(ies)

1. Name(s) _____ Age _____
2. Address _____ Spouse Name _____
3. Principal or employer at time of accident _____
4. Address _____ Agency facts _____
5. Liability insurance _____ Coverage _____
6. Adjuster _____
7. Injury claims _____
8. Property damage claims _____

C. Accident Facts

1. Date and time _____
2. Place _____
3. Description of vehicles a. (client) _____
                              b. _____
4. Driver's name, age and address a. _____
                                    b. _____
5. Owners' names and addresses a. _____
                                 b. _____
6. Passengers' names, ages and addresses a. _____
                                           b. _____
7. Witness' names, ages, and addresses _____

_____

8. Driver drinking or disability _____
9. Injuries known to other persons _____
10. Statements of adverse party(ies) at scene _____
_____ later _____
11. Statements of client at scene _____

_____ later _____

12. Road conditions _____ Weather conditions _____

13. Road width _____ lanes _____ direction _____ posted speed _____

14. Traffic controls _____ a. _____

                           b. _____

15. Speed and direction of vehicles a. _____

                           b. _____

16. How accident occurred _____

_____

_____

_____

17. Position of vehicles after accident a. _____

                           b. _____

18. Location and extent of damage to vehicles: a. _____

                           b. _____

19. Location and description of collision debris _____

_____

20. Skid mark location and length a. _____

                           b. _____

21. Damage to objects other than vehicles _____ Description _____

_____

Which vehicle inflicted _____

22. Diagram of accident:

D. Personal Injuries of (Client) (Adverse Party)

1. Description of injuries _____ _ _____

_____

2. When injuries first noticed _____

3. How removed from scene _____ Where to _____

4. Emergency treatment _____ Where given _____

Who treated _____

Description of treatment _____

_____

Condition of patient after treatment _____

5. Where hospitalized _____ Dates _____

6. Treating doctors a. _____ b. _____

Address a. _____ b. _____

Phone a. _____ b. _____

Specialty a. _____ b. _____

Description of treatment a. _____

b. _____

Dates of treatment a. _____

b. _____

7. Description of present complaints and disability _____

_____

8. Future medical treatment and estimated cost _____

9. Medical reports obtained _____

10. Medical reports to get _____

E. Special Damages

1. Medical expenses: (check if bill received)

Hospitals and charges a. _____ b. _____ c. _____

Doctors and charges a. _____ b. _____ c. _____

_____

Dentist and charges _____

Private nurse and charges _____

Medication expenses _____

Ambulance _____

Miscellaneous (identify) _____

2. Medical bills paid to date and who paid _____

_____

3. Estimated future medical expense (identify) _____

4. Insurance coverage (hospitalization, medical insurance, auto medical payment) _____

_____

5. Estimated loss of earnings _____

Employer's name, address and phone _____

Job classification and duties _____

Amount and basis of compensation _____

Verification of earnings loss _____ from whom _____

6. Estimated future loss of earnings _____

7. Impairment of earning capacity _____

Part-time job _____ Employer's name, address and phone _____

Estimated loss of part-time earnings _____ basis _____

Other reduction in earning power (explain and estimate) _____

8. Expense of outside employment for job or home due to disability _____

_____ who employed _____ estimated expense _____

F. Property Damage

1. Owner client's vehicle _____ address and phone _____

Where taken after accident _____ by whom _____

Where vehicle now _____ repaired or salvaged _____

Who repaired _____ address and phone _____

Cost of repairs _____ have itemized bill _____

If total loss who bought salvage _____ price _____

When and where vehicle purchased _____ price _____

If not repaired, garages estimating and amounts _____

_____

2. Collision insurance coverage _____

   Deductible _____

   Adjuster name, address and phone _____

   Status of collision claim _____

3. Rental of substitute vehicle _____ From whom _____

   Rental cost to date and rate _____ Necessity of _____

   Estimated value of loss of use _____

4. Other involved vehicles a. _____

   b. _____

   Owner name, address, and phone a. _____

   b. _____

   Driver name, address, and phone a. _____

   b. _____

   Estimated repair cost a. _____

   b. _____

   Where vehicles taken after accident a. _____

   b. _____

   Insurance company and adjuster a. _____

   b. _____

5. Property damage other than vehicular _____

   Owner name, address, and phone _____

   Description and extent of damage _____

   Estimated repair cost _____

G. Police and Other Agencies' Involvement

1. Names and employer of policemen investigating _____

   _____

2. When arrived at scene _____ Who called _____

3. Describe police investigation _____

   _____

4. Alterations at scene before police arrival _____

5. Client interviewed by police _____ where and when _____

Statement taken _____ Oral or written _____ Have copy _____

6. Other drivers interviewed by police _____ where and when _____

Statements taken _____ Oral or written _____ Have copies _____

7. Witnesses interviewed by police _____ where and when _____

Statements taken _____ Oral or written _____ Have copies _____

8. Arrests _____ Who arrested _____ Charge _____

Court appearance date _____ Disposition _____

9. Police photographs _____ Have copies _____

10. Police accident report made _____ Have copy _____

11. Private ambulance used _____ Company _____ Driver _____

Describe involvement _____

12. Tow truck used _____ Company _____ Driver _____

Describe involvement _____

Debris swept from road _____

H. Miscellaneous

1. Conversation of client with other drivers _____ When and where _____

_____

Relate verbatim _____

_____

_____

2. Claims of others in client's family _____

Names and addresses _____ Relationship to client _____

Description of personal injuries _____

Present medical expenses _____ bills _____

Present complaints _____

Estimated future medical expenses _____ disability _____

Loss of services to spouse _____ Describe _____

_____

Loss of consortium to spouse _____ Describe _____

_____

3. Past settlement discussion _____ Who with _____

Describe and summarize _____

_____

_____

Settlement offer _____

4. Attorneys representing adverse parties _____ Names, addresses and phone ____

_____

5. Medical authorization forms obtained from client _____

6. Employer authorization form obtained from client _____

7. Instructions given client _____ Summarize _____

_____

_____

8. Fee contract executed _____ Contingent _____ % Hourly___ $ ___
    Retainer $ _____

How To Use This Client Interview Form

This form covers most of the information you must obtain from your client the first time you interview him after agreeing to take his case. Reproduce these questions on letterhead or legal-size paper by mimeograph or some other method, and then fill them out as completely as possible as you interview your client.

Your objective, of course, is to get all of the *relevant* information, so use these questions as guidelines, omitting and adding to them as needed for each particular case.

A client interview checklist for divorce or legal separation cases begins on page 116.

Client Interview Checklist For Divorce Or Legal Separation Case

A. Client—Personal

1. Name _____ Age _____
   Address _____ Phone _____
2. Residences during marriage (approximate dates) _____
   _____

3. Prior marriage _____ Dates of _____
   Prior spouse name _____
   Place and date of termination _____ Reasons _____
   _____

4. Date and place of present marriage _____
5. Education _____
6. Personal property owned by client:
   Bank accounts _____ Sole or joint _____
   _____ Present balances _____
   Stocks and bonds (indicate "s" for sole, "j" for joint) _____
   _____
   Vehicles _____
   Other (omit clothes and personal effects) _____
   _____

7. Real property owned by client: _____
   Address and description _____
   Interest owned _____ Who owns other interest _____
   Estimated present market value _____
   Mortgagee _____ Present balance _____
8. Total value of client's property _____
9. Present employment _____ Position _____
10. Monthly income _____ Earnings _____ Other _____
11. Indebtedness (name of creditor and amount owed; mark "j" if joint)
   _____
   _____
   _____
   _____ Total _____
12. Monthly payments on indebtedness (By creditor and amount)
   _____
   _____
   _____
   _____ Total _____

13. Monthly living expenses (Kind of expense and amount; average)

_____

_____

_____

_____ Total _____

Expense exhibits obtained _____

14. Antenuptial agreement _____ Copy obtained _____

15. Name and address of Next Friend if client is Minor _____
_____ Relationship _____

16. Previous divorce actions between parties (date of, court where filed, disposition and reasons for) _____

_____

17. Prior attorneys representing client _____

_____

18. Close relatives in area (name, address and relationship) _____

_____

_____

19. Religion _____

B. Spouse—Personal

1. Name _____ Age _____
   Address _____ Phone _____

2. Present Employment _____ Position _____
   Monthly income _____ Earnings _____ Other _____

3. Personal property owned individually (nature of and estimated value) _____

_____

_____

4. Real property owned individually (nature of, address and estimated value) _____

_____

5. Individual indebtedness (name of creditor and amount owed) _____
   _____ Total _____

_____

6. Monthly payments on indebtedness (By creditor and amount) _____

_____ Total _____

7. Estimated monthly living expenses (Kind of expense and amount) _____

_____

_____

8. Monthly support paid to client _____

9. Prior marriage _____ Dates of _____

Prior spouse name _____ Place and date of termination _____

_____

10. Offensive habits _____
11. Present physical or mental abnormalities _____
12. Criminal convictions _____
13. Threat to client, children and/or property _____
14. Attorney representing spouse _____

_____

15. Religion _____

C. Children

1. Names _____ Ages _____
   Addresses (if other than client's) _____
   _____
2. Natural or adoptive _____
3. Preferences of older children as to custodian _____

   _____

4. Present physical or mental abnormalities _____

   _____
   _____

5. Monthly payments by or to client for support of _____
6. Client's children from prior marriage _____ Age _____

   _____
   _____

   Support paid or received from prior spouse for support of _____
7. Spouse's children from prior marriage _____ Age _____

   _____
   _____

   Support paid or received from prior spouse for support of _____
8. Religion (if other than client's) _____

D. History of Marriage

1. By whom married _____ Church _____
2. Reasons for marriage _____
3. If separated, when last lived together _____ Where _____
   Who left home _____ Why _____
4. Describe course of marriage _____

   _____

5. Specific complaints about spouse _____

_____

6. Dates, places, and events causing marital difficulty _____

_____

_____

_____

7. Prior separations _____ Describe (Date, place, and reasons for)_____

_____

8. Prior counselling _____ Dates and names of counsellors _____

_____

E. Reasons For Interview

1. Recent events (Dates, places, and detailed description) _____

_____

_____

_____

2. Grounds for divorce and/or legal separation _____

_____

3. Names and addresses of witnesses (relate to grounds) _____

_____

_____ Friendly or unfriendly _____

_____

4. Client's preference: divorce or legal separation _____

5. Immediate threat to client, children, or property _____
   Explain threat _____

F. Remedies Indicated

1. Divorce _____ Legal separation _____
2. Temporary alimony _____ Permanent alimony _____
3. Property division _____
4. Temporary child support _____ Permanent child support _____
5. Injunction, preliminary and/or permanent _____
6. Temporary restraining order _____
7. Restoration of prior name _____ Name desired _____
8. Attorney fees, temporary and/or final _____ Amount _____
9. Subject of injunction (other than spouse) _____
   Purpose of _____

G. Reconciliation Possibility

1. Client love spouse _____ Spouse love client _____
2. Conditions under which client will reconcile _____
_____
3. Counselling desired by client _____ By spouse _____
Counsellors acceptable to client _____
_____To spouse _____
_____
4. Attitude of client toward marriage _____
5. Attitude of spouse toward marriage _____
6. Reconciliation effort desired by client _____

H. Miscellaneous

1. Documents client to submit _____
_____
_____
2. Evidence client to obtain _____
_____
_____
3. Other instructions to client _____
_____
_____
4. Office meeting with spouse _____ When _____
_____
5. Office interviews with witnesses _____ When _____
_____
_____
6. Fee contract: flat rate $ _____ hourly rate $ _____ per hr.
retainer $ _____

GETTING THE DOCUMENTS, REPORTS, AND RECORDS YOU NEED

It is a rare case that can be won without documentary evidence and a common case that will be lost without it. Do you seek money for personal injuries or property damage based on tort? Then you'd better have accurate wage records; medical, hospital, and drug bills; car title or real property deed, repair estimates; bills, etc.

Do you claim breach of a purchase agreement for a house? You need the original or duplicate original of the agreement, written proof of tender of the deed or purchase money, and any correspondence about the non-performance.

There are needed documents associated with every type of case you are likely to handle. A bit of thought and effort during the client interview will usually identify the issues you must prove to win, the documentary evidence you must secure to prove those issues, and the documents the client can produce.

> **ACTION RULE:** Arrange to secure all relevant documents in the possession or within the reach of your client during the initial interview.

THREE BENEFITS OF ARRANGING FOR DOCUMENTATION AT THE INITIAL INTERVIEW

1. You get whatever documents the client has in his possession and avoid the risk of loss or destruction, either accidentally or because he did not know they were important.
2. You get documents that the client does not have in his possession but can secure before their custodian destroys or misplaces them (e.g., employer records; accounts, bills, estimates, or correspondence in the hands of client's spouse, agent, etc.)
3. Early possession of essential documents permits early negotiation and, often, an early settlement.

OBTAINING CLIENT AUTHORIZATION FOR PROTECTED REPORTS AND RECORDS

In addition to documents a client has or can get, there are other writings, often vital to victory, that you should get yourself. But to get them requires written authorization from the client, for they are reports or records in the hands of third persons, shielded against disclosure.

The shield takes various forms. It may be the bar of privileged communications, as where the third person is the client's doctor, lawyer, or accountant. It may be the institutional privilege of a hospital, clinic, employer or a governmental agency.

Examples of Reports And Records Requiring Client Authorization

1. Case records possessed by client's previous attorney.
2. Income tax reports and business records possessed by client's accountant.
3. Records of case histories, office visits, and treatment possessed by client's doctor and dentist.
4. Case reports prepared by client's doctor and dentist at your request.
5. Wage, dispensary, and personnel records possessed by client's employer.
6. Hospital or clinic records pertaining to services rendered client.
7. Probation and parole records on client possessed by Court or State.
8. Tax records pertaining to client possessed by Federal, State, or Municipal governments.
9. Unemployment compensation records relating to client, in the custody of a State agency.
10. Motor vehicle accident reports filed with a State agency and involving client.

You'll derive much the same benefits from early acquisition of reports and records as from obtaining legal documents at the first chance. The risk of loss, misplacement, and destruction of vital papers is no less real because the custodian is a professional, institution, government agency, or corporation rather than the client himself. And certainly the prospect of an early and favorable settlement is just as bright.

> **ACTION RULE: Instruct client to deliver immediately those documents in his possession or in the possession of third persons who will surrender to him. Have him sign sufficient forms authorizing you to obtain protected records and reports. Then submit the authorizations without delay.**

How To Get Protected Papers Quickly

As soon as you complete the client interview checklist, review it in the client's presence to determine the documents, records, and reports that may be of value to your case. Then, with the client's help, make a list of those papers he has in his possession or can obtain quickly.

Instruct him to deliver such documents to your office before a definite date (as early as reasonable) and to notify you immediately if any document is unobtainable for any reason. Prepare the list in duplicate, giving one copy to the client and attaching the other to your interview checklist. Then instruct your secretary to remind you on the delivery date to check for receipt of all documents. (If any are missing on that date, find out why!)

Prepare a second list, in the client's presence, of all records and reports that *may* be of value to your case for which written authorization is required. Have the client sign as many of the appropriate authorization forms as needed (one form for each custodian) *plus several extra forms of each type,* and mail an authorization form to each custodian with a cover letter requesting the specific record or report wanted. Be sure to promise payment for whatever "reasonable" fee may be charged for duplicating the record or preparing the report.

Follow up the authorization form with a further letter (a phone call is better unless it's too costly) whenever a record or report is not received in due course.

SAMPLE AUTHORIZATION FORMS FOR YOUR USE

Figures 1-1 and 1-2 are standard authorization forms that will serve you quite well. Figure 1-1 covers dental, medical, or psychiatric records—and reports from dentists, physicians, clinics and hospitals. Figure 1-2 is generic and adaptable to many other custodian requests.

AUTHORIZATION FORM FOR MEDICAL, DENTAL, PSYCHIATRIC AND/OR HOSPITAL INFORMATION

TO:_____ RE: _____

This is to authorize any physician, psychiatrist, dentist, clinic, hospital, medical attendant, or others to furnish my attorney,_____, any and all information that he may request regarding my physical, dental, or psychiatric condition, and treatment rendered; and to allow him to see, copy, or order copies of any X-rays or records which you may have regarding my condition or treatment. My said attorney has been retained by me to prosecute a claim against another/others for injury sustained and your full cooperation with said attorney is respectfully requested.

You are further requested to disclose no information to any other person without written authority from me to do so. All prior authorization is hereby cancelled. I hereby waive any privilege I have respecting said information to my attorney.

_____

STATE OF _____, COUNTY OF_____,

Sworn to and subscribed in my presence this____day of _____, 197_.

_____
                                    Notary Public

Figure 1-1

AUTHORIZATION FORM FOR GENERAL INFORMATION

TO:_____ RE: _____

   This is to authorize you to furnish my attorney,_____
_____, any and all information which
he may request pertaining to_____
_____
and to allow him to see, copy or obtain copies of any report
or record which you have in your possession. My said attorney
has been retained by me to represent my interests in a pending
matter and your full cooperation with him is respectfully
requested.

   You are further requested to disclose no information to
any other person without written authority from me to do
so. All prior authorization is hereby cancelled. I hereby waive
any privilege I have respecting said information to my
attorney.

_____

STATE OF_____, COUNTY OF_____,

   Sworn to and subscribed in my presence this___day of
_____, 197_.

_____

         Notary Public

Figure 1-2

HOW TO MAKE THE CLIENT DO PART OF THE WORK

There is an old story about a telephone call from a frantic mother to her doctor. "Doctor," she cried, "my baby just swallowed a bullet. What should I do?"

"The first thing is," replied the doctor, "don't point him at anybody."

Now your clients are not babies; bullets are not cases, so when you have a client with a case, point him ... point him ... point him! Point him in directions you wish him to take as the case progresses, toward duties he can and should perform to help build his case and help you win it.

> **ACTION RULE:** Tell the client at the initial client interview that you will ask him to perform certain duties from time to time as his case progresses. Exact a clear promise from him to perform them promptly when asked, as a condition of your taking his case. Review the following checklist of client duties with him and assign those tasks which he can begin working on now.

Checklist of Client Duties

1. Obtain names and addresses of witnesses (neighbors in divorce and trespass actions; other affected persons in nuisance cases; character witnesses in criminal defenses).
2. Assist in arranging interviews with witnesses.
3. Keep track of witnesses as the case progresses (check on their whereabouts from time to time so you can produce them when needed).
4. Obtain documents and memoranda or copies of them.
5. Assist you in tracing documents and memoranda so you can obtain them.
6. Assist in identifying reports and records.
7. Assist in obtaining protected reports and records when the custodians or preparers refuse or delay submitting them.
8. Assist with any phase of your fact investigation upon request.
9. Visit the accident or crime scene or the scene of any material event to familiarize himself with it and the surroundings.
10. Attend all court proceedings punctually and in proper attire.
11. Attend depositions (his own or another) punctually.
12. Assist in preparing answers to interrogatories.
13. Attend conferences in your office or elsewhere on request.
14. Adjust his manner and method of answering questions according to your dictates.

15. Maintain records as the case progresses according to your instructions (medical and drug expenses, changes in physical condition; nature and amount of continuing damages; itemization of living expenses).
16. Take photographs of objects and scenes when requested.
17. Submit to medical and other tests when requested.

Three Bonuses From Putting Clients To Work

More than the obvious benefits of building evidence and helping you with work emerge from this practice of assigning tasks to clients. They become actors rather than observers and their morale is boosted. They see first hand the complex work involved in any case, better appreciate your role and more readily concede the fee charged is your due.

Finally, working clients are more willing to accept the necessary delays involved in whipping a case into shape for the best settlement or trial. They see good reasons for the delays.

One delay for which there is no good reason is any delay telling your client what is expected of him. Tell him at the initial interview and make it clear that your further representation depends on his *total* cooperation.

HOW TO INSTRUCT THE CLIENT FOR
THE PROTECTION OF YOUR CASE

Admitting the wisdom of all clients in coming to you for service, for some of them it will be the last wise thing they do in their cases. Unless you anticipate and prevent it, they will act in ways that damage your chance of winning—and disturb your relationship with them. They will hurt you not because they are stupid or perverse, but because they are untutored in the wiles of claims agents, legal investigators, and other opponents who may set traps for the unwary. So you must tutor them!

For example, nearly all clients talk too much about their cases outside their immediate families, never realizing that neighbors are often questioned by investigators under subterfuge. Maybe that genial chap on the next bar stool is the opponent's investigator digging for impeachment. Also, injury claimants repeatedly disregard advice of their doctors, never realizing their medical progress is slowed, the doctors offended, and their cases jeopardized.

Divorce clients often carry on torrid love affairs under the eyes of their estranged spouses, causing settlement negotiations to founder and grounds to disappear.

> ACTION RULE: Besides telling your client at the initial interview what you require him to do (Client Duties) state what you require him not to do. Use the following checklist as a reminder of subjects to cover.

CHECKLIST OF CLIENT "DON'TS"

1. *Don't discuss any aspect* of your case outside your immediate family unless I authorize it.
2. *Don't submit any written statement or sign any document* pertaining to your case unless I authorize it.
3. *Don't discard any papers* (documents, correspondence, memoranda, bills, or records) relating to your case without my permission.
4. *Don't exaggerate your claims* (feigning illness, injury, or disability).
5. *Don't minimize your claims* (saying you feel fine when you don't; telling friends your marriage is O.K. when it is not).
6. *Don't act in any way inconsistent* with your claims or defenses (don't be seen in bars if you are a defendant in a drunk driving case; don't play golf if you claim a painful disability).
7. *Don't get arrested,* even for a traffic violation.
8. *Don't antagonize the adverse party* wilfully (don't boast to others about what your lawyer will do to him, or vilify him to a common acquaintance).
9. *Don't browbeat or bribe witnesses* (don't tell them they *must* cooperate or else; don't offer them more than expenses to come to my office for an interview, and not even expenses unless I authorize it).
10. *Don't call me repeatedly* for status reports. I will notify you when anything significant to your case occurs. Call if you must, but only if a month or more has passed without hearing from me.
11. *Don't ask me for a loan.* The canons of my profession prohibit my lending you money. If creditors bother you, tell me. I will write them explaining your situation and urging patience.

WHY AND HOW TO EVALUATE THE CLIENT AS A WITNESS

Whether you represent a claimant or defendant, an important determination you must make in every case is its settlement value. In a civil case, this means the minimum sum or remedy you will accept or the maximum you will give; in a criminal case, it is the most serious offense you will plead to, if any.

Settlement value is primarily based upon a prediction you must make to answer this question: *Assuming my case was tried to a jury or judge tomorrow and considering all factors known to me which bear on the trial outcome, what is that outcome likely to be?*

The factors bearing on trial outcome are many; they are discussed in detail in Chapter 7. Now, your job is to zero in on *one* of these factors—how effective a witness your client will be.

Since the client is almost always your most important witness, it's little wonder that the fortune of your case largely rests upon him, and upon his person, not just his testimony. *A jury and judge weigh and credit testimony as much by a witness's appearance and manner of speaking as by what he says—sometimes more so!*

Example: A Client Who Spoke The Truth And Was Not Believed.

An assault and battery case was tried in my court sometime back in which a police chief of a small village was accused of breaking the plaintiff's jaw in an unprovoked attack. When the plaintiff took the stand the jurors visibly shuddered. He was the typical hippie—greasy hair down his back, unkempt beard, clothes looking like they had been slept in, etc.

He told his story straightforwardly enough. He had been in a bar drinking beer when the chief entered and ordered him out. He demurred, the chief grabbed his arm, he pulled away, and was punched in the mouth.

As he testified he looked defiantly at the jury as though expecting disbelief, and he was short-tempered and impolite on cross-examination.

When the defendant took the stand, comparison was inevitable. The chief was resplendent in his spotless uniform. His manner was polite, his attitude righteous, and his testimony believed. He responded to a complaint of a disturbance, he said, the plaintiff was unruly, swung at him and he, the chief, used only such force as was necessary to subdue him. The jury was out a half hour and returned a verdict for defendant.

But the story has an interesting epilogue. Some weeks later plaintiff's lawyer produced an affidavit from a respected local citizen who was out of town during the trial. The affidavit confirmed plaintiff's story in every detail. I granted a new trial which plaintiff won.

Now plaintiff might not have won the first trial even had he looked and spoke like a choir boy. But surely the odds of his winning would have been much better.

Why is it that appearances sometime outweigh truth in the battle of persuasion? Emerson explains it best: "Moral qualities may rule the world but at short distances the senses are despotic."

> ACTION RULE: As soon as you finish the client interview and he has gone, complete a Witness Evaluation Checklist by indicating where the client falls in each category. Preserve the checklist for your future determination of settlement value.

Figure 1-3 is a checklist form you can use for all witnesses interviewed, the client and others.

WITNESS EVALUATION CHECKLIST

Physical Appearance: impressive_____ average_____ unimpressive _____
repellant _____

Personal Grooming: immaculate_____ good _____ average _____
slovenly _____

Manner of Dress: orderly_____ disorderly _____

Manner of Speech: very clear & coherent _____ mostly clear & coherent _____
mostly incoherent _____
wordy_____ terse _____

Speech Abnormality: none _____ heavy accent _____moderate accent _____
physical impediment _____

Command of English: excellent _____ good _____ fair _____ poor _____

Personality: personable _____ outgoing _____ introverted _____
grouchy _____ argumentative _____

Appearance of Sincerity: entirely sincere _____ mostly sincere_____
mostly insincere_____unbelievable _____

Fact Retention: excellent _____ good _____ fair _____ poor_____

Apparent Intelligence: above average _____ average_____
below average_____ dull _____

Receptivity to Instruction: very receptive _____ fairly receptive _____
resistant _____ unmanageable _____

Summary of Evaluation: excellent witness _____ good witness _____
fair witness _____ poor witness _____

Issue(s) Witness Testimony Tends to Prove or Refute: _____
_____
_____

Strength of Proof: Extremely strong _____ Strong _____
Moderate _____ Weak _____

Remarks: _____
_____

Figure 1-3

Interviewing Friendly And Unfriendly Witnesses

TABLE OF CONTENTS

2

Interviewing Friendly And
Unfriendly Witnesses

"Luck happens when preparation meets opportunity."
Anonymous

Section A.   INTERVIEWING THE FRIENDLY WITNESS

This is a witness who owes some allegiance to your client by a relationship to him, either family, employment, social, or affection. You begin your interview with a built-in bias favoring you and should exploit it vigorously.

You will be surprised occasionally by a client's relatives who react like Mr. Micawber's ... with utter indifference to his needs. But this is the exception that tests the rule. Most people who are in a position to help will do so—given direction—so long as it does not cost them anything.

FIVE INTERVIEWING OBJECTIVES
FOR THE FRIENDLY WITNESS

Economy of effort and time make knowing your interview objectives vital. Have them all in mind when you see the witness the first time, since there is no time like the first time for achieving them. There may not be a second. Even if you can and do hold a second interview, his memory will not be in the same mint condition as it was before.

1. *Enlist his active and partisan support for your case.* He comes to you almost as a volunteer for duty. Explain his importance to the case and the client's chance of winning it. Explain the merits of the client's cause, his "right" to victory, and the anticipated opposition; then tell the witness what he must do to help overcome the latter to achieve the former.

2. *Obtain and preserve all favorable facts.* Both from the client's interview and your preliminary investigation, you should have a fairly complete grasp of the facts you must prove to win your case. Establish all you can through friendly witnesses during their interviews, then make certain you can do so again at a later settlement conference or trial.

3. *Obtain and subordinate unfavorable facts.* Knowledge of "bad" facts is as important as knowledge of "good" facts, for in a legal setting knowledge is indeed power—power to convert favorable facts to favorable evidence and so prove your essential issues, and power to anticipate unfavorable facts and either extenuate, dilute, or refute them. But after knowledge comes use. And it is the favorable facts, not the unfavorable, you want your friendly witness to use subsequently ... in his statements to you and your opponent. You must orient the witness in his partisan role by emphasizing his facts that help your case and by subordinating (not suppressing) those that hurt it. Techniques for accomplishing this orientation are discussed in Part III of this Guide.

4. *Obtain leads to other facts, evidence, and witnesses.* Like Galahad's quest for the Holy Grail, the treasure a lawyer seeks (decisive, winning evidence) often can only be found by pursuing leads friends supply. So, a friendly witness may not himself be the eyewitness you need, but with patient probing, he may supply you with clues to that witness's identity and whereabouts.

5. *Obtain sufficient personal data about the witness so you can locate him whenever necessary later.* A good witness who cannot be produced when needed is as much use as a million dollars that cannot be spent. Expectations count for very little at the negotiating table. When interviewing such a witness, believe that he will disappear ten minutes after leaving your office. Then gather enough personal information about him so you can trace him if he does.

With these important interviewing objectives in mind, consider the following rules and techniques for achieving them.

WHEN AND WHERE TO CONDUCT THE INTERVIEW

With rare exception, friendly witnesses are willing to come to your office for their interview. Some will be reluctant to inconvenience themselves. But most all will consent if you insist, and of course you should insist.

The office is familiar ground to you and alien ground to him. You are the sovereign, he is a commoner, as evidenced by your desk and swivel (throne) and his chair (supplicant's bench) before you. He is also impressed by you and your role as champion of his friend.

Most importantly, you have his entire attention, free from interruptions and distractions that waste so much of your time and lower the quality of the interview.

Do not repeat the mistake so many lawyers make of interviewing a friendly witness at his or the client's house. They think an advantage of gratitude is gained by deferring to the witness' convenience. Rubbish! All advantage is lost. These office factors, which collectively loosen a witness' tongue and make him ready to please, are missing in a living room.

CHECKLIST FOR SETTING UP A FRIENDLY WITNESS INTERVIEW

1. *Identify all friendly witnesses* from the client interview and immediately phone them for office interviews. Impress them with the necessity of coming in at the earliest possible date and time convenient to your schedule.
2. *Get help from the client* for the recalcitrant witness who does not want to get involved or does not want to do it at your office.
3. *Interview the witness at his home or office only as a last resort,* in those few instances when he is afflicted or adamant, and is too important to ignore. But ask for privacy during the interview itself and insist upon it. Otherwise you will share his attention with family or business colleagues, and the share you get will not be worth having.
4. *Schedule the interview during regular office hours unless it is impossible* for a witness to leave job or family. Generally the claimed impossibility is actually a personal inconvenience which will be accepted if required. Do require it. More than your convenience is involved. On occasion you will want your secretary to take shorthand notes during the interview. Also, there are times when a few phone calls to public or private offices will verify, refute, or modify significant facts the witness supplies. These must be placed during the day, and should be made in his presence so he willingly adjusts his facts when necessary.

   FOR EXAMPLE: The witness swears it was raining at the time of the accident and the streets were wet, while your client said the day was clear and streets dry. A phone call to the local weather station can usually determine which is true. The false memory should be willingly erased by whichever witness possessed it, but this will only happen if he learns his error from the official source.

5. *Schedule all friendly witness interviews* from which the facts elicited will probably prove or contribute to prove an essential issue in your case *within several days of the client interview.* Speed is essential so that you reach the witnesses 1) while they are available; 2) before your opponent does; 3) while their memories are fresh, and 4) while there is time to pursue leads to other evidence with which they may supply you.

6. *Interview each friendly witness separately* and not as a part of a group session. Some lawyers I know hold collective interviews, a few from laziness, others on the rationale of group therapy (they help each other cure individual defects). It is a bad practice. For in the process of conforming to each other's memory of facts, they make their testimonies carbon copies of each other. Stories that tend to correspond not only perceptually but verbally will be received skeptically.

7. *Interview each witness outside the presence of the client,* who places a constraint upon the witness, interfering with truth. The witness is not completely free to tell you what he believes happened if it expresses or implies blame of the client.

HOW TO MAKE A LUKEWARM WITNESS INTO A BURNING SUPPORTER

There is an ancient proverb that carries a modern truth: "If you wish to enlist a man to your cause, show how it profits him." Paraphrased slightly, the statement applies to witness interviews:

"If you wish to enlist a man to your cause, show him how it profits someone close to him."

ACTION RULE: Begin your interview by explaining the merit of your client's case, why he deserves to win it and what the client can expect to gain if he does win. Then impress the witness with his importance in achieving that goal. Tell him with utmost sincerity that he is vital to the client's victory. If the witness can tend to prove some essential issue, it is impossible to exaggerate his importance. You must build up his self-image so he does all he can to build up your case.

By definition, a friendly witness has a committment to the client stemming from family, social, employment, or friendship ties. You start with a favorable bias. But both committment and bias start out as negative qualities—he will not knowingly do anything to hurt the client.

The degree to which this witness will actively help your client depends on answers to three questions: How much will his help benefit the client? How much will it benefit *him*? How much will it cost *him*? The answers you supply to these questions will determine whether you have an indifferent helper who volunteers nothing, or a zealous helper, eager to contribute all he can toward victory.

How Not To Begin

Interviewing lawyers may be gathered into four main categories: "Lawyer Perfunctory," "Lawyer Indifferent," "Lawyer Horse Shedding" and "Lawyer Evangelist" according to the way they habitually begin witness interviews.

Lawyer Perfunctory: Good afternoon, Mr. Smith. You were a passenger in my client Goodwin's car when he had his accident, weren't you? What can you tell me about the accident that will help Goodwin's case?

Lawyer Indifferent: Mr. Smith, isn't it? You're here to tell me all you know about the Goodwin accident. (places microphone in front of witness) The easiest way to handle this is for you to talk into this microphone for a tape recording. Just tell me everything you know about the accident. While you're doing that I'll just go over some papers for a case I have in court tomorrow. (The lawyer opens a file cover and begins reading as Smith starts speaking; "I got up that morning at eight o'clock and had breakfast with my wife, Sarah. I remember she had a bad headache . . . .")

Lawyer Horse Shedding: (For those readers unfamiliar with this beguiling term, "horse shedding" is a euphemism for telling a witness what to say when he would otherwise say something quite different. Its modern and less picturesque equivalent is "subornation.")

Good morning, Mr. Smith. I think right off we ought to agree about something important. We both want Mr. Goodwin to win this case, right? Good. And I think you'll concede that my expertise and experience qualify me to decide what it's going to take to win it, right?

Now then, I've talked to Goodwin and made a preliminary investigation. This is the way I think the accident happened. See if you can't agree that this is what happened.

Goodwin was travelling West on Six Mile Road at a speed of between 40 and 45 miles per hour, next to the center line, when all of a sudden this other car driven by Billings veered across the center line . . . . (Smith seems about to interrupt, changes his mind and nods his head.)

How You Should Begin A Witness Interview

Apart from the obvious defects in their techniques, these lawyer types give no attention whatever to a vital ingredient of an interview . . . witness warm-up. This is analogous to the audience warm-up prior to many television shows. The "second banana" cracks jokes for five minutes before air time to get the audience in the proper frame of mind.

Similarly, a friendly witness should be put in the proper frame of mind at the outset of his interview, which is to say he should be motivated to give all possible help to your cause. He must become eager to help far beyond the motivation of his natural bias; to volunteer, to cudgel his brain for recollections, to aid the search for evidence and to remain "on call" and ready at any future date.

The surest way to warm him up is to enlist him in a crusade. Here is a scene that should occur more often than it does:

Lawyer Evangelist: Good afternoon, Mr. Smith. Thank you for coming. You know I represent Mr. Goodwin. My job is to obtain an adequate sum of money for him to pay his bills, protect him against future bills, and pay him something for the pain he's had.

I think he's entitled to every dollar he gets. As far as I can tell he was in the right and the other driver, Billings, was in the wrong. But it's not just a matter of money, as important as that is. It's a matter of justice. Mr. Goodwin had a right not to be injured by somebody's carelessness. One good way to curb driving carelessness is to file a claim against the driver and his insurance company. That's what we've done in this case.

Mr. Smith, you're a key man in this case. We need your help. As a passenger in Goodwin's car you were in a good position to see what happened. And since you're not a party in the case your words will carry much weight.

I think there's a chance of winning a substantial amount of money for Mr. Goodwin. But only if we can have your help. Are you willing to help us? (I'll help in any way I can," says Smith.) Not just by coming here and answering questions. I may ask you to help in the investigation or talk to the lawyer for Billings and tell him what happened. Would you be willing to do these things knowing that they will help our case? (Smith nods vigorously.)

Good. Now I'm going to ask you questions about the accident. Listen closely and answer them to the best of your recollection. If you don't understand a question, tell me. All right? (Witness nods.)

Where were you when you began riding in Goodwin's car the day of the accident? . . .

This is a sample script. Choose your own words appropriate to each case, but stick to this format. Make the witness aware of his importance and you give him a stake in your fight; he becomes an ally who is only slightly less hungry for victory than you yourself.

MAKING SURE YOU ARE THOROUGH

While most lawyers are quick to resent the suggestion that their interviewing techniques are not unique and original, there are in reality only two basic interviewing styles, narrative and question and answer. There are, of course, blends of the two in different ratios that some find comfortable.

Why The Question And Answer Style Is Better

The preponderance of able lawyers I know employ the question and answer interviewing technique. It ensures the fullest possible disclosure of facts by directing the witness' attention to areas of information you need to know in order to achieve the five objectives previously discussed. Asking a witness to "tell you all he knows about what happened" is an invitation to a rambling discourse as wasteful of your time as it is difficult to follow and record. It is like a shooting match in which the contestant is never told where the target lies.

Five W's And An H

The importance of obtaining all useful information at the first interview is even more acute with a witness than with a client. The latter is readily accessible to you. The former is often not.

Newspaper reporters, who live in dread of an incomplete interview, devised a bit of doggerel as a reminder of the scope of their questions:

> Who, what, when, where, why, and how.
> Get the answers to each right now.

These questions pretty much cover the essentials of any witness interview. They translate for our purpose into the following:

WHO   —is the witness? (All significant personal facts)
       —were the participants in the event he witnessed? (Names and addresses)

WHAT —is the event he witnessed, together with prior and subsequent events having a bearing on it?

WHEN —did the major and subordinate events he witnessed occur?

WHERE—did the major and subordinate events occur, and where were he and the principals then?

WHY —did the major and subordinate events happen as they did? (Opinion of causation and fault)
—were he and the principals at the places of the events? (Statement of reasons)
—did the principals act as they did? (Opinion of motivation)

HOW —did the major and subordinate events occur? (Explanation and/or opinion of the mechanics of events)

> **ACTION RULE: Prepare a witness interview checklist form for each type of legal case you regularly handle or use the general purpose form supplied here. Print a supply adequate to your needs and use a form for every witness interviewed. If you use the checklist in this Guide, strike out blanks that are clearly inapplicable, then be sure all other blanks are filled. Consider what unique facts not covered by the checklist may be helpful in your specific case and add the needed questions to the list.**

Figure 2-1, which begins below, is a witness interview list that can be easily adapted for use in a wide variety of adversary cases; automobile injuries to warranty breaches, equitable remedies to criminal defenses.

CHECKLIST FOR A WITNESS INTERVIEW

File # _____ Client _____

A. Personal

1. Date _____ Place of interview_____
2. Name_____ Address_____
3. Marital status_____ Age _____ Phone_____
4. Spouse name_____ Employer_____
5. Witness employment, present and past _____
_____ Business phone_____

6. Relationship to client_____

7. Names and addresses of parents, brothers and sisters _____

_____

_____

8. Arrests and convictions (felonies and serious misdemeanors)_____

_____

9. Present health_____ Past mental illness _____

10. Hearing defect_____ Visual defect_____

Corrective appliances_____ Worn at time of events_____

B. Events Witnessed—Automobile Accident

1. Date and time_____ Place_____

2. Position of witness at time of accident_____

_____

3. Description of vehicles_____ a. (client)_____
   _____ b. _____

4. Drivers names_____ a._____
   _____ b. _____

5. Passengers names__ a._____
   _____ b. _____

6. Other witnesses_____ Names and addresses_____
   _____ Where positioned _____

7. Speed and direction of vehicles   a._____
   _____ b._____

8. Vehicle movements to point of accident___ a._____
   _____ b._____

9. Road conditions_____ Weather conditions_____

10. How accident occurred_____

_____

_____

11. Statements of drivers after accident   a._____
    b._____

12. Statements of other witnesses _____

13. Position of vehicles after accident___ a._____
    _____ b._____

14. Location and extent of damage to vehicles   a._____
    b._____

15. Location and description of collision debris _____

16. Skid marks location and length___ a. _____
    _____ b._____

17. Opinion of fault _____

18. Statement of police officer (s)_____

19. Possible unidentified witnesses_____ Suggestions to locate_____

20. Injuries and damage observed_____

21. Diagram of accident:

C. Events Witnessed—Divorce

1. How long known client and spouse_____

2. Circumstances of acquaintance_____

_____

3. Knowledge of client character and reputation_____

_____

4. Knowledge of spouse character and reputation_____

_____

5. Wife care and treatment of children_____

6. Husband care and treatment of children_____

7. Observed course of marriage_____

_____

_____

8. Wife behavior toward husband_____

9. Husband behavior toward wife_____

10. Opinion of wife as housekeeper_____

11. Opinion of husband as provider_____

12. Wife's personal habits_____

13. Husband's personal habits_____

14. Dates, places and events of observed marital trouble_____

_____

15. Other witnesses to above events_____

_____

16. Pertinent statements of wife_____

_____

17. Pertinent statements of husband_____

_____

D. Events Witnessed—Criminal

1. How long known client_____

2. Circumstances of acquaintance_____

3. Knowledge of client's character and reputation for truthfulness_____

_____

4. Knowledge of client's character and reputation for honesty _____

_____

5. Knowledge of client's character and reputation for peaceableness_____

_____

6. Basis of above-stated knowledge_____

_____

7. Knowledge and source of knowledge about alleged crime_____

_____

8. Events witnessed_____

_____

_____

9. Date, time and place of events_____

_____

10. Other witnesses to same events_____ Names and addresses_____

_____ Where positioned _____

_____

11. Knowledge of complainant_____Circumstances of_____

_____

12. Statements of client overheard_____ When, where, and to whom_____

_____ What said _____

_____

13. Statements of other witnesses overheard_____When, where, and to whom _____

_____ What said_____

_____

14. Statements of complainant overheard_____ When, where, and to whom_____

_____What said_____

_____

15. Police investigation observed_____When and where _____

    Describe _____

_____

16. Statements of police overheard _____ When, where, and to whom _____
_____ What said _____

_____

17. Possible unidentified witnesses _____ Suggestions to locate _____

_____

18. Diagram of events witnessed:

```
┌─────────────────────────────────────────────────┐
│                                                  │
│                                                  │
│                                                  │
│                                                  │
│                                                  │
│                                                  │
│                                                  │
│                                                  │
│                                                  │
└─────────────────────────────────────────────────┘
```

E. Events Witnessed—Miscellaneous

1. How long known client _____

2. Circumstances of acquaintance _____

3. How long known opposing party _____

4. Circumstances of acquaintance _____

5. Connection with case _____

_____

6. Events witnessed _____

_____

_____

7. Date, time and place of events _____

_____

8. Other witnesses to same events _____ Names and addresses _____
_____ Where positioned _____

9. Statements of client overheard _____ When, where, and to whom _____
_____ What said _____

_____

_____

10. Statements of other witnesses overheard _____ When, where, and to whom _____
_____ What said _____

_____

_____

11. Statements of other party overheard _____ When, where, and to whom _____
_____ What said _____

_____

12. Relevant documents or physical objects possessed_____

_____

_____ Where presently located_____

_____

13. Claimed injuries and/or damage observed_____
    When and where first observed_____
    Describe_____

    _____

14. Possible unidentified witnesses _____Suggestions to locate_____

    _____

15. Significant value of witness not covered_____

    _____

16. Remarks_____

    _____

17. Diagram of events witnessed _____

┌───┐
│   │
│   │
│   │
│   │
│   │
│   │
│   │
└───┘

There is more that friendly witnesses can do for your case than supply you with facts. They can also supply you with investigative manpower. And given the motivation you have excited in them for your client's cause, most will do whatever they can . . . if only you ask.

Put these witnesses to work developing leads to new evidence, protecting the quality of their own evidence.

THREE PROFITABLE REQUESTS YOU SHOULD MAKE AT THE CLOSE OF THE INTERVIEW

1. *Ask the witness to help you in any specific phase of your fact investigation that can be handled by a layman without hazard or expense.* There are innumerable small but essential tasks he is qualified to do. For example, in a divorce case he or she may help the client prepare documentation of monthly expenses and cost of necessities, or even

supply surveillance of the opposing party—where the client cannot because of identification and you will not because it is unseemly. In an automobile accident case, the witness may be assigned the job of tracing the other vehicle to a garage or junk yard so photographs can be taken.

2. *Ask the witness to discover the identity or whereabouts of other witnesses.* Does he tell you during his interview an unidentified resident nearby the accident scene might have witnessed it? Ask him to canvass the neighborhood in search of the witness. Explain the importance of the search and he will do it—and probably turn up the witness.

3. *Ask the witness to notify you whenever he is contacted for a statement by opposing counsel or representative, so you can arrange to be present. Also tell him not to discuss the case until you are present.* Of course you cannot ethically refuse your opponent access to the witness. But you can, quite ethically, delay or postpone the interview until you can make the scene. And you should do it. Some lawyers and many insurance adjusters and private investigators are adroit with "Have you stopped beating your wife" questions, and artful in slanted editing of written statements. You have the right to protect the witness from doubletalk, doublethink, and doublewrite.

How Witness Sleuthing Can Bring Victory

Two cases come to mind in which asking friendly witnesses to help in the investigation paid off. The first involved a divorce action. The wife knew her husband was "stepping out" but could not learn with whom and to where. Though surveillance was obviously called for, the wife could not do it all herself and could not afford a private investigator.

So the lawyer asked his client's sister to "follow Sam." After a two-week effort, she not only traced Sam to a sleazy motel 20 miles away but also took photographs of Sam's car parked next to the motel sign, Sam himself emerging from a room, and Sam's paramour hanging all over him.

The second case concerned a two-car intersection accident in which both drivers claimed the green light, and in which there were no known eyewitnesses. A gas station stood at one corner, but when plaintiff's counsel questioned the two attendants who had been on duty that night, both denied seeing or even hearing anything. The lawyer was unconvinced.

It happened that plaintiff's neighbor and personal friend was a regular patron of the station. He was asked, and readily agreed, to question the attendants himself in a low-key way. It took him all of three days (a brake job, oil change and a lot of gas) to produce the eyewitness that eventually led to a substantial settlement.

Never suspecting a link between his good customer and the lawyer, one attendant told a beautiful story. While pumping gas that night he heard tires squeal, looked up and saw plaintiff's car skidding into the intersection, with the green light, and against the side of the other crossing car.

HOW TO GUARANTEE WITNESS AVAILABILITY WHILE THE CASE PENDS

How common and how piteous is the bleat, "I have a terrific witness who'll win the case for me . . . only . . . he's disappeared and I can't find him."

Many lawyers regard witnesses as money on deposit . . . always available in case of need . . . and promptly forget about them after the interview. Then, usually months later, when need arises, the lawyers are dismayed to learn the accounts are closed. The witnesses have left for parts unknown.

Demographers tell us that America is a mobile and motorized society in constant flux. The average stay of a family at a residence location is between five and seven years. Using six years as the median and averaging out, it means that 12½ percent, or one out of eight witnesses, will move from his present address within 18 months, which is approximately the average docket delay—filing to trial—in American general jurisdiction courts.

These statistics translate into a grim message for lawyers. A significant number of witnesses will be missing when they are most needed. Some of them will be easily traced, to be sure. But others will not be traced at all in the absence of care. For personal or financial reasons, these emigres (more like escapees) deliberately hide their tracks, leave no forwarding address, "fold up their tents . . . and silently steal away."

Gaining The Means Of Discovering Witnesses At The Interview

A few simple precautions during the witness interview will give you the means of locating most witnesses if they suddenly perform vanishing acts.

ACTION RULE: Obtain all the personal information about each friendly witness during his interview, using Part A of the Witness Checklist. At the end of the

interview, ask the witness to notify you promptly of any change of residence, employment, or telephone number. Then, during the pendancy of your case, call him every 2-3 months (your secretary can do it) to maintain contact.

The friendly witness is a cooperative fellow and genuinely wants to help; at least he wants to help at the time of the interview. Here is the rub; the friendliness may disappear due to a later estrangement between client and himself, and if the witness moves away a great distance, he may easily feel that returning for some event in the case is both too costly and too inconvenient. So he moves without notice and remains hidden without remorse.

Remember: Even though a witness qualifies as "friendly", always interview him with the expectation that he will disappear sometime during the pendancy of your case and you will have to track him down.

MAKING THE FRIENDLY WITNESS MORE EFFECTIVE AND EVALUATING HIM

That someone qualifies as a friendly witness because of some relationship to the client, either family, employment, social, or friendship, does not make him a better witness. On the contrary, the qualification makes him a worse witness. It is a stigma rather than a medal to those whose evaluation of him determines the size of your settlement, trial victory, or defeat.

> **ACTION RULE: The "First Law Of Witness Credibility" is that the credibility of a witness varies inversely to the closeness of the relationship between client and witness, and to the degree of benefit his testimony confers upon the client.**

This means that any testimony tending to benefit your client will be less persuasive the closer his relationship to the witness.

CREDIBILITY CHART FOR FRIENDLY WITNESSES

This table shows various relationships your witness can have with your client. They are listed in descending order—from most credible to least.

1. Witness is a stranger riding in client's car at the time of accident.
2. Witness is a mere business or neighborhood acquaintance with irregular contacts.

3. Witness is a social acquaintance with irregular contacts.
4. Witness is an acquaintance who belongs to the same church.
5. Witness is a fellow employee with frequent contact (ride in the same car to and from work or eat lunch together).
6. Witness is a frequent social interactor (they belong to the same lodge, club or fraternal organization).
7. Witness is a satellite relative (niece, nephew, aunt, uncle, etc.)
8. Witness is a business or professional colleague whose income is affected by client's work.
9. Witness is a close personal friend.
10. Witness is a close relative (husband, father, son or brother).

Within this range, you can usually place the witness you are interviewing, and then you can prepare him according to the credibility problem indicated.

How "The Credibility Gap" Can Hurt!

Since the favorable statements of a mere neighbor are often met with skepticism, those of a near relative require even more care to obtain credibility. I remember an assault and battery trial pitting brother against brother. Al defended the charge that he had struck brother Bob with a hammer at a family barbeque.

After testifying on direct examination to the assault itself, Bob made some helpful admissions during cross-examination. He had been drinking heavily, he said, and baiting Al unmercifully. Several epithets were exchanged of the kind reflecting on parentage (an odd thing in the case of brothers). Then came the apparent clincher for the defense.

Under pressure from counsel, Bob grudgingly admitted hitting the defendant before being struck in turn.

"He was holding the hammer and I guess he just struck at me without thinking after I hit him," he said.

To the astonishment of everyone, especially the prosecutor, the jury returned a verdict of guilty. Later when asked to explain the verdict in the light of Bob's admissions, the jury foreman said:

"We didn't believe Bob. After all, he's the defendant's brother and everyone knows that brothers will lie for one another."

Defense counsel looked bewildered. "Well if you didn't believe the brother," he asked, "why didn't you reject his statement about being hit by the hammer?"

"I said brothers will lie *for* one another," replied the foreman. "They won't lie *against* each other."

How To Minimize Future Skepticism By Preparation At The Interview

As with most rules of thumb, the one concerning witness credibility is subject to exception. The degree of discredit attaching to statements of friendly witnesses is significantly affected by the appearance of truth-telling. The more there is of the latter, the less there is of the former. Your job, then, is to enhance this truth-telling appearance to the optimum for each friendly witness on whom you rely. The time to begin that job is at his interview.

> **ACTION RULE:** Before asking the witness to recite facts concerning the accident, incident, or event, always emphasize that you wish him to be fair and accurate in such recital. Make it clear that you do not want to hear just those facts favoring the client but the facts adverse to him as well.

Unless you tell friendly witnesses you want a full and accurate story, you will get an expurgated one—purified, perfumed, and powdered to show off the client to best advantage. Having told the edited version once, he will tell it twice . . . and so on . . . until it soon contains the whole truth to him. But it will contain no truth to others!

On the other hand, start him off with the truth, containing pluses and minuses just as truth does, and you prepare him to neutralize (in part) the skepticism of those you wish to persuade . . . opposing counsel and party, insurance company, referee, judge, etc.

Admitting little faults in order to persuade of large virtues is a surefire case selling technique you should use. Does the air-conditioner salesman say Brand A has it all over B and C? You dismiss it as puffing. But what if he says A is inferior to B and C in one of seven categories, although superior in the other six? Well, now, that's different.

Evaluating The Witness' Potential

Be sure to appraise each friendly witness in terms of his likely effectiveness at trial—immediately after his interview, when your memory of him is freshest and judgment is most certain.

ACTION RULE: After instructing the witness concerning his statement of facts and completing a Checklist form on him, fill out a Witness Evaluation form (see Chapter 1). Make sure that all blanks are completed while his statement, attitude, manner, appearance, etc. are fresh in your mind, and preserve both forms for later use in assessing the settlement value of your case.

Section B. INTERVIEWING THE UNFRIENDLY WITNESS

THE OBJECTIVES OF AN UNFRIENDLY WITNESS INTERVIEW

Now you are dealing with a witness owing some allegiance to the adverse party, including the adverse party himself. Someone with an inherent bias favoring the other side because of some relationship between them, either family, employment, social or affection, is likely to be unfriendly to you and your cause.

That that someone is a witness and theoretically spurred by a sense of justice and yen for fair play means nothing. He will say and do whatever he can to help his ally beat you . . . within reason. Within reason? This is the qualification that offers lawyers the chance to deal effectively with these witnesses.

Taking Advantage Of His Scruples

As with the populace generally, some adverse witnesses are basically dishonest. They are so in the habit of lying that they lie on all subjects great and small. They rarely pose a problem for the opposing lawyer, for, making no effort to be plausible, they are soon found out.

The techniques of this section are designed for the bulk of witnesses who are basically honest and want to appear honest to others.

ACTION RULE: The large majority of adverse witnesses you interview will state the whole truth about any event until they learn which facts favor your client and which favor their friend. If the interview takes place after they have learned the difference, they will conceal the first and exaggerate the second, but only so long as they do not thereby reveal themselves untruthful.

Six Interviewing Objectives

Armed with knowledge of these tendencies, interview an adverse witness with these six objectives in mind:

1. *Interview him before he acquires a factual slant—before he learns which facts hurt and help his ally.* The witness will perceive the value of some facts without being told. He does not need an attorney to tell him that driving on the wrong side of the road and misrepresenting features of a house for sale are facts favoring persons injured by those acts. But he does not know legal principles relating to either event to appreciate the refinement of factual advantage. Was the driver forced over the center line? Was the misrepresentation innocent? You must get to the witness before opposing counsel teaches him the refinements and prepares him against your coming.

2. *Obtain and preserve all favorable facts.* The witness is more likely to disclose facts helpful to your side at this stage of the case than at any other. When he does, you must be prepared to preserve them in some form usable later in settlement discussions. (Forms and techniques for preserving witness statements are presented in Chapter 6.)

3. *Obtain and preserve unfavorable facts.* Getting an early recital of all facts the witness knows damaging to your client confers three benefits: 1) You learn your opponent's evidence—and can conduct your investigation and preparation accordingly; 2) Having stated all unfavorable facts he knew, the witness cannot subsequently add to them without the threat of impeachment and discredit; 3) The witness cannot later correct obvious errors in his interview disclosures to harmonize with discovered truth without the threat of impeachment and discredit.

4. *Establish his adverse bias and the factual basis of it.* Of course, if the witness is the adverse party, his identity is enough. Similarly, his spouse and close relatives bespeak relationships that presume bias. But other relationships do not create the same presumption even though bias is evident. That the witness is the adverse party's employer does not mean his word will be disbelieved. But if his income is affected by the party (override on sales commissions) or there is a close social intimacy as well, his value as a witness sharply diminishes. Such detail is vital to your successful disparagement of unfriendly witnesses.

5. *Obtain leads to other facts, evidence, and witnesses.* It is not only his version of the events he witnessed you should seek and can get. The witness will often know of witnesses, documents, or physical objects important to the case you never knew existed. Interview him before he is warned against helping you, probe for such leads, and then be pleased at the number you get.

6. *Obtain and preserve impeaching utterances.* Establishing a bias in the witness favoring the adverse party gives you a weapon. But couple that with a glaring untruth he stated and you hold an explosive sufficient to

blow credibility right out of the witness. Always seek to induce at least one such untruth in every interview, then preserve it in statement form for later use.

The balance of this Chapter supplies techniques for achieving these witness objectives. They carry no warranty against failure. But they succeed for other lawyers and they will for you . . . if only you employ them.

GETTING A HELPING HAND FROM THE ADVERSE PARTY

Of all unfriendly witnesses, the least friendly and the most important to interview is the adverse party himself. Yet the majority of lawyers shun him, as if he carried a virus—or a gun. Though he carries neither of these, he does carry facts; informative, beneficial and impeaching facts.

> **ACTION RULE: As long as the adverse party is not represented by counsel it is no violation of professional ethics to interview him and you should do so. Ask him at the outset of your interview whether he retained counsel. If he did, then learn counsel's name, address, and phone number and leave immediately. But if no counsel has yet been hired, even if he is about to do so, then proceed with the interview as you would with an unfriendly, non-party witness.**

Of course, if you are employed to defend against a lawsuit already filed or after an attorney notice letter was received by your client, you have no chance to interview the other side. But if you enter the case before either one occurs (generally the case when representing claimants and often the case when retained by their opponents) nothing but indolence, procrastination, or misunderstanding stands in your way.

There is no guarantee of a successful interview. There never is with unfriendly witnesses, who have been known to swing doors and fists in lawyers' faces. But like winning race car drivers, winning lawyers take great risks for great gains. And there are no greater gains imaginable than those stemming from favorable or impeaching utterances from adverse parties.

A Belligerent Response That Backfired

Sometimes a door in the face pays off better than a courteous interview. One able lawyer I know, representing an electric utility accused of damaging a nearby residence with fly ash, sought to interview the owner at his house.

He took the precaution of having a shorthand reporter with him (See Chapter 6).

The owner met him at the front door, about six feet two inches, two hundred fifty pounds, and all of him saturated with beer. The lawyer introduced himself and his purpose politely. He just wanted to find out what happened and to see the damage. Whereupon the owner launched into a flood of abuse and invective that would have brought the reporter's hands to her ears . . . if she had not been so busy writing.

With every question the fury intensified. No s-o-b from that company would set foot on his property. He was going to sue for a million dollars and not be satisfied until it closed its (blankety blank) doors.

The interview was transcribed with each obscenity intact. Soon after, the owner hired a lawyer and suit was filed. The very first negotiating session between the lawyers resulted in settlement for a very modest sum, because as soon as plaintiff's counsel read the interview transcript, he realized the impact it would have on judge and jury. Betrayed as a greedy, drunken boor, his client would surely lose the sympathy he naturally relied upon.

The Helpful Results Of A Courteous Approach

The above example is the exception, not the norm. Approach the adverse party in a courteous, low-key manner, and you can usually expect an equally courteous response. At most you will obtain facts of *positive* value (facts supporting your claims or defenses); at the least you will obtain facts of *negative* value (inconsistent or contradictory facts to his claims or defenses).

It is said the secret of Napoleon's success is that he always struck where the enemy was strongest, so that if he made a gain there, victory usually followed. Your opposing party is his own strongest witness. Make a gain there and your victory, too, will often follow.

WHEN, WHERE, AND HOW TO INTERVIEW UNFRIENDLY WITNESSES FOR BEST RESULTS

A short order cook once told me that most people live their entire lives without knowing how to fry an egg, even though they may eat eggs every day. It is the same thing with many lawyers and hostile witnesses. They either pass them over altogether as unfit for questioning, or dash about interviewing them with little forethought and no art. Small wonder, then, that these lawyers spend their entire professional lives convinced that nothing of value can be extracted from the unfriendlies.

Four Plateaus Of Interviewing Effectiveness

Able lawyers know that the manner in which they deal with these witnesses often dictates the success or failure of their case. This is obvious, since the extent to which adverse witnesses can prove claims of their own party, or disprove claims of yours, determines the case outcome.

Dealing effectively with them requires that you interview them effectively. And to do this you must achieve four plateaus: *Get access to them; get them to talk to you; get utterances from them that help your case,* and *put these utterances into a form that you can use subsequently.*

Here is a checklist of techniques that will help you reach each plateau. Each has been pre-tested by use and accomplishment. Employ them in your practice and see if your results are not better than before.

INTERVIEWING CHECKLIST FOR UNFRIENDLY WITNESSES

1. *First, identify by name and address* the adverse party and other unfriendly witnesses whose testimony, according to information on hand, is likely to prove or disprove essential issues in your case. Information from your client, friendly witnesses, police reports, newspaper accounts and other early sources of facts provides the identification.
2. *Interview these witnesses* within a week after the identification is made, in order of their potential importance to the case—the adverse party first. Delay of even one day may see a lawyer hired. Interview the most important witness first because this is the order in which your opponent will visit and prepare them against you.
3. *Conduct the interviews yourself* whenever possible. If this is impossible, then use only an associate or investigator whose interviewing ability has been demonstrated.
4. *Interview the witnesses at their homes* during the evening or weekend. Do not call for an appointment first nor give prior notice of your coming. All witnesses are reluctant to submit to a lawyer interview, and

unfriendly witnesses most of all. Call for an appointment and it will be refused. Give them advance notice and they will tell you to stay away, not answer the door or leave before you arrive. Explain that you are "out this evening investigating events that concern them" to take some of the sting from your seeming rudeness. That will get you to the next item of procedure.

5. *Identify yourself truthfully* as the lawyer for "so and so," and never dissemble yourself or mission. Say you are trying to learn all the facts of the case, no matter whom they hurt or help, and that you must investigate fully before you can decide whether, and on what basis to settle it. Be courteous and friendly. Never threaten, bluster, or "throw your weight around." The witnesses will probably talk to you about the events now, if only to justify and promote their perspective.

6. *Obtain sufficient personal information* about the witnesses to establish the relationships between them and the adverse party—and the factual basis of their biases.

7. *Ask the witnesses first to narrate the events they witnessed.* Then question them specifically about each such event. A narration will occasionally disclose helpful facts that detailed questioning will overlook ... and vice versa. The dual approach requires repetition and targets discrepancies caused by poor memory, poor articulation, uncertain conviction, increasing candor, heightening partisan goal awareness, and just plain mistakes. Whatever the cause, discrepancies taint witness credibility and are important to you.

8. *Tell the witnesses about favorable facts you know* that contradict or are inconsistent with unfavorable facts he has stated and ask if they want to change these portions of their stories. Sources of such favorable facts may be police reports, official documents, disinterested witness statements, friendly witnesses, and your client. Obviously, the more authoritative and disinterested the source of your facts the greater the pressure upon unfriendly witnesses to conform their own.

9. *Take a shorthand reporter along* to the interviews whenever the witness potential or client's purse warrants the fee (it will vary from about $35 to $100 depending on time, distance, locale, and reporter). There are occasions when you will not have the time or freedom to write up a statement of witness utterances and the reporter is your surety of future use. A stenotype reporter is preferable to none at all, but less valuable than a shorthand reporter because some witnesses are intimidated to silence by the unfamiliar machine.

10. *Make your own notes of significant portions* of witness utterances, especially those that benefit your case. Make them briefly and

discretely, because the witnesses will surely be alarmed by the sight of furious writing.

11. *Whether a reporter accompanies you or not,* always write out a concise memorandum of witness utterances in his presence, using statement writing techniques presented in Chapter 6. Give the memorandum to him for review and correction. Have him sign or otherwise authenticate it, using techniques outlined in the same chapter. Make an original only and do not supply the witness with a copy unless he insists.

HOW TO INDUCE IMPORTANT IMPEACHMENT

Up to now we have emphasized one of two main objectives of an unfriendly witness interview . . . the eliciting of probative facts (facts tending to prove either the adverse party's claims or defenses or your own). Now for the second main objective, when his probative facts are, as is commonly true, substantially unfavorable to you: the eliciting of impeaching facts (facts tending to impair the validity of the probative facts or his credibility in stating them).

It is true that the objectives are the same when you cross-examine an unfriendly witness at trial. And you may succeed in eliciting both kinds of facts then. But the purpose of this Guide is to show you how trials can be avoided, by winning more and better settlements sooner. Pre-trial impeachment of adverse witnesses is one big way in which good settlements are made.

How Witness Impeachment Caused A Settlement

Nick Rossi is a 72-year-old Italian-American from Buffalo who, two years ago, agreed to purchase ten acres of prime residential land for $100,000. When the day of performance came and went without the money in escrow, the owner called Nick for an explanation.

The deal was off, said Nick, claiming that *since he could not read English* he did not understand the terms of the purchase agreement. He thought he was buying the land for $60,000, not $100,000, which he said was far more than the land was worth.

The seller argued to no avail. Since he did not know Nick personally, nor did he see him sign the agreement, he did not know whether the claim of illiteracy in English was true or false. Realizing a lawsuit was in the offing, seller hired an able lawyer, who almost immediately paid a surprise visit to Nick's home and interviewed him.

Nick repeated his claim to the lawyer, and it was confirmed by his married daughter who lived with him (she moved in one week after the agreement was signed). Although he had lived in America forty years he never bothered to learn to read English. He said he had taken the real estate agent's word that the agreement called for $60,000 and signed where he was told (the agent denied this, but since he had a $6,000 commission and his license on the line, his word was of dubious value).

The lawyer suspected Nick and his daughter were lying—but how to prove it? There was no test he could use and the fact that Nick spoke English meant nothing. He went over the agreement line by line, asking Nick to read the words he understood out loud. But the old man was not caught. He looked the document over blankly until he reached the signature lines, then said "Nick Rossi" brightly.

Then the lawyer hit on the right approach. He would not meet the claim head-on, but indirectly. Evidencing an interest in the man's history, he invited Nick to talk about himself. Visibly relaxing, Nick responded with gusto and for the next half hour spun a detailed autobiography, his daughter filling in with facts from time to time.

The lawyer left with an eight-page statement containing the following facts about this self-proclaimed English illiterate: Nick was a retired restaurateur, owning and operating three spaghetti houses in Buffalo over a twenty-six year span until three years before. He negotiated and closed the leases at all three locations himself, hired and paid his help, purchased supplies, paid bills and prepared menus . . . all with only intermittent help from his daughter. *And he was a naturalized American citizen for 22 years,* having taken his first papers in 1942 and his oath in 1948.

No judge or jury in the world would believe Nick's claim in the face of such a history, a fact his subsequently hired lawyer soon conceded after reading the statement. The case was settled for a $500 reduction in the purchase price (which the agent was more than willing to take off his commission).

Six Forms Of Verbal Impeachment

The impeachment accomplished in the Rossi case exemplifies one of six forms which verbal impeachment may take. Here are the six, illustrated by a hypothetical complainant in a robbery case.

1. *Inconsistent utterances.* Complainant says he positively recognized defendant as the robber. Later he says that within two hours of the robbery he viewed six men in a police line-up, defendant included, and was unable to make a positive identification.
2. *Contradictory utterances.* Complainant first says the robber was about six feet tall wearing a blue sweater. Later he says he was about medium height wearing a blue jacket.
3. *Implausible utterances.* Complainant says he positively identified defendant as the robber even though he viewed him from 500 feet away.
4. *Irreconcilable utterances.* (present in the Rossi interview) Complainant says he had a clear view of defendant's face as he ran towards him following the robbery. Later he says the robber wore a broad billed cap pulled low so it masked his face.
5. *Perceptual defect.* Complainant says he wears prescription lenses for nearsightedness, later admits he was not wearing them at the time of the robbery.
6. *Discrediting facts.* Complainant says he positively identified defendant as the robber at the scene. Later he says that two days later police pointed defendant out to him at the police station, saying he was "the man who did it."

TECHNIQUES FOR GETTING AND KEEPING IMPEACHMENT

First of all encourage the witness to tell his story in detail and show interest in all he says. Never be impatient because he draws it out. The more he talks, the greater the likelihood he will impeach himself in some way.

Be as receptive to the unfavorable facts he relates as to the favorable. If you cut him off with an "I didn't ask you about my client's speed. I want to hear about your driver's speed," you offend him, increase his suspicion, cheat yourself of facts you should know and destroy any chance of impeaching him.

Ask the witness to repeat the essentials of his story at least twice. Your pretext for asking is that you wish to make full and accurate notes. Few witnesses can repeat a detailed observation identically. Often the differences are enormous and serious impeachment, taking the form of contradiction, inconsistency, implausibility, or irreconcilable facts (occassionally all four) results. The secret here is to accept an implausible statement impassively, note it and move on to another subject. Never express astonishment, doubt or disagreement and never ask him to repeat it. Give the witness any hint he said something wrong and he will re-examine and probably correct it.

Encourage exaggeration. Damaging statements can sometimes be completely discredited by exaggeration to the point of absurdity. For example, defense counsel in a divorce case interviewed plaintiff wife's sister and asked about defendant's habits. "He drinks a lot" . . . "Did you see him drunk?" . . . "Oh, yes, quite a lot" . . . "Every time you saw him?" . . . "Yes, I'd say so." Counsel secured a written, signed statement from the witness in which she says, "Tom is always drunk." From "drinks a lot" to "always drunk" is some progression, moving from a reasonable statement of fact to an implausible defamation prompted by witness bias.

Note irreconcilable facts in the witness story without comment, as you would an implausible statement. Never tip him off that a conflict exists in his facts and, most importantly, never ask him to explain it. It is shameful how often lawyers free skewered witnesses from their hooks. If the witness tells you he saw your client's face at the crime scene, then later says client's back was turned the whole time, leave it be. Bury both facts in a written statement and get it signed. Never say, as many lawyers would, "Tell me, Mr. Martin, how could you see my client's face if his back was turned to you all the time," because he will answer "Oh, he turned his face toward me one time and I got a good look."

Observe whether the witness wears glasses or a hearing aid. If so, ask his lens prescription, visual ratio, auditory setting and name and address of his prescribing doctor, company or technician. Ask if he was wearing his appliance at the time of events he witnessed. (A later check of any optician, optometrist, opthamologist, or ear specialist will establish the extent of his impairment.) Finally, in a criminal defense case, always ask the witness about his contact with police; when and where he saw them, what happened, what he said, and what he was told. Much of what an eyewitness believes he perceived of an event is often supplied (intentionally or unwittingly makes no difference) by police suggestion and information. (A common occurrence in the case of an eyewitness is for police to show him two or three mug shots of "suspects", defendant among them. The slightest suggestion of guilt is often all it takes to draw a positive identification from a badly confused witness.)

How Bad Technique Can Hurt You

Singling out one bad practice from many is a little like treating one wound and ignoring ten others. But I remember a lawyer telling me how a single interviewing lapse cost him a good settlement.

He represented plaintiff in an auto accident case. Injuries were modest, but there was evidence defendant had made no effort to avoid the collision after seeing plaintiff stopped in front of him.

Counsel interviewed defendant before filing suit: "Tell me how the accident happened," he asked. "I was eastbound on Lake Shore Boulevard at about 6 p.m. and I was *blinded by the setting sun*," defendant replied.

Quite without realizing his blunder, the lawyer threw away his impeachment advantage . . . "How could you have been blinded by the sun," he blurted. "You were going east and the sun sets in the west."

"Oh, that's right," said the startled defendant, looking quite sheepish, like a small boy caught telling a whopper. He thought for a moment, then looked up brightly.

"Then it must have been the sun reflecting off cars ahead of me because it sure was bright."

By challenging the witness, not only did the lawyer lose strong impeachment but he aroused a latent suspicion in the witness that the lawyer sought to catch him in a mistake. So he refused to sign any statement whatever.

Not surprisingly, some months later at the pre-trial conference, defendant's counsel argued the reflecting sunlight claim with gusto. The case was settled for a modest sum, far less than the amount plaintiff's lawyer knew he would have won had he possessed the impeaching statement, creating, as it did, clear inferences of deceit and reckless driving.

REMEMBER: getting impeachment from an unfriendly witness is only half the chore. You must preserve it in a written statement or court reporter

record for use in settlement negotiations. React to an impeaching utterance as a poker player reacts to a drawn ace . . . without a flinch or a murmur. The pot will be larger in both cases.

MAKING CERTAIN YOU LEARN ALL THE "GOOD" FACTS

You can be sure that an unfriendly witness possesses more than just unfriendly facts. No case is ever so cut-and-dried that something good cannot be said for both sides. And the witness can say something good for you if he wants to.

Of course, he never wants to. He is biased in favor of the other side and will not wittingly say anything damaging to his ally. The key word here is "wittingly". Your objective must be to get him to disclose facts which damage the ally unwittingly (the witness will never say his friend was speeding, but you may get him to say that he was going about 55 m.p.h., which you know is in excess of posted speed limit).

Here are some techniques that will help you induce those unwitting disclosures.

CHECKLIST FOR GETTING FRIENDLY FACTS
FROM UNFRIENDLY WITNESSES

1. *Know your case as thoroughly as possible when you commence the interview,* so you have in mind favorable facts disclosed by others. Read your completed client interview and friendly witness interview forms and statements, police reports, and other pertinent material in your possession beforehand.
2. *Use the cross-examining style of questioning . . . but gently.* There is no judge around to enforce rules of evidence, so phrase your questions in a manner that assumes the answers you want. Do not say, "Was M driving about 55 m.p.h.?" Instead say, "Wasn't M driving about 55 m.p.h.?" a subtle but persuasive change of phrasing, as any experienced trial counsel knows. Neither is a judge around to compel the witness to answer your questions. Your interview is not by right or invitation but by his sufferance, so do not be aggressive in your style. If he refuses to say "Yes" to your speed question, let him have his way. Say, "What speed was he travelling, then?" He is likely to answer, "No more than 50 m.p.h.," which may still be over the speed limit.

3. *Ask for facts and not conclusions.* Do not say, "Didn't M fail to yield the right of way?" or "Didn't J act in self-defense?" Instead say, "Didn't M drive into the intersection without stopping for the stop sign?" or "Didn't P throw a punch at J just before J struck him?"

4. *Refer to facts from authoritative sources that conflict with his facts in an effort to change his mind.* If the witness said your client was drunk and the police report has an "x" opposite the phrase, "No sign of drinking," show him the report, and then ask if his opinion may not be mistaken.

5. *Ask the witness about favorable facts you know, but he has not disclosed.* If you learned from another witness that the robber spoke with a southern accent and you know your client does not, ask the complainant detailed questions about what the robber said and how he said it. Try for an admission—at the very least—that his accent was not native to your area.

6. *Prod him for facts you suspect he knows but has not disclosed that are likely sources of advantage.* A passenger in the adverse party's car can tell you about distractions existing in the car prior to the accident; conversations, car radio, cigarette lighting, etc.; whether windshield wipers were working, the windshield dirty . . . and other such details. A next-door neighbor in a divorce case will know much about the couple's personal habits, public manner with each other, condition and appearance of the children, etc. The complainant in a criminal case will know the lighting conditions when the crime occurred, his own state of mind, times, distances and what was said.

7. *Ask the witness to show you any pertinent documents in his possession.* In a contract case, ask the adverse party to see his copy of the contract and examine it for writing not appearing on your copy. Also ask for his copies of correspondence exchanged between himself and your client, paying special attention to originals from the client of which he may not have made copies.

8. *Ask him to repeat any conversations he may have had with your client, the adverse party and any other witness concerning events at issue.* These will often confirm what your client has told you and/or contradict the adverse party and other unfriendly witnesses, since the interviewee does not know what the others have or will tell you.

9. *Ask each unfriendly witness other than the adverse party whether he spoke with opposing counsel. If so, get full details of the conversation, when, where and what was said. Was he interviewed personally? Give a written statement? Did that statement deviate from the facts he has given you? In what particulars? What did your opponent tell him about the case?*

There are three purposes for these questions. First, you should always know the facts your opponent has to work with. Second, the witness will sometimes disclose different facts that were told opposing counsel than were told you, then must admit he was mistaken to one or the other of you. The third purpose is to distinguish coaching from honest recollection. If pressed the witness will occasionally admit that your opponent fed him facts . . . . "Well, he just reminded me of a few things I'd forgotten". Find out all about those "things" and include it in your written statement.

10. *Finally, ask the witness if there is anything he would like to add to what he has told you.* It is surprising how often this question strikes a vein of untapped lore. I remember asking it of the complainant in a burglary case. "You didn't ask me about the fingerprints of your client the police found," he said. "They found prints on the window that was jimmied open."

This was the first I had heard about prints being found, so I went to the prosecutor to confirm the identification, fully expecting to arrange for a plea of "guilty" on the best terms obtainable. He admitted finding prints but refused to say whether they matched the defendant's. A court order was quickly secured requiring the police to disclose comparison results. The answer was *they did not match!* A *nolle prosequi* soon followed. A case was won because of an innocuous question to a hostile witness . . . "Do you have anything to add"?

HOW TO EVALUATE THE UNFRIENDLY WITNESS

As regards hostile (unfriendly) witnesses, more than impeachment must be considered in evaluating them. What damaging facts do they possess and how damaging are they? What favorable facts do they have and how favorable are they? What about their appearance, personalities, fact retention, and communication abilities? Good, bad, or average?

All of these factors must be worked into the equation to determine whether witness "x" equals a substantial negative influence on your case value, a moderate influence, or no influence at all. Determine it you must, for as has been said earlier and will be said again later in this Guide, *you cannot negotiate good settlements consistently unless you determine each case's settlement value beforehand.* And to do this you must evaluate each important factor which bears on settlement value. An unfriendly witness is one such factor.

The "Balance Sheet" Method

Here is a mathematical method of witness evaluation that an able lawyer I know has used for years, and swears by. It proceeds by assigning a numerical value to each factor bearing on the witness' probable effectiveness, then draws certain conclusions about the witness based upon value totals. The method contributes objective standards to what has traditionally been a most imprecise and subjective function.

For most lawyers, evaluating witnesses as an act of deliberation is simply never done. Few would think to sit down, review witness statements and records, consider personality and appearance profiles and determine each witness' probable effectiveness for and against him. The real value, then, of this evaluation method is that it requires a detailed analysis of each witness and allows a rule of thumb measure of his effectiveness that can easily be worked into the larger calculation of case settlement value.

How To Do It

1. *Complete a witness evaluation form* (See Figure 1-3) reflecting the witness' appearance, personality, etc., as soon as possible after his interview.
2. *List the essential issues of your case* in column form in the center of a page of paper:
   >   defendant's negligence
   >   proximate cause (defendant's negligence)
   >   plaintiff's negligence
   >   proximate cause (plaintiff's negligence)
   >   injury
3. *Review the witness' written statement* (or your notes if no statement was obtained or a court reporter was present) for unfavorable facts relating to each issue
4. *Assign a numerical weight* from 0 to 4 to the left of each issue on the page according to the tendency of his facts to prove or disprove it (0 means no proof, 1 slight proof, 2 moderate proof, 3 strong proof, and 4 conclusive proof).
5. *Assign a numerical weight* from 0 to 4 to the left of the issue column representing your opinion of the witness' superficial qualities as shown by his evaluation form.
6. *Review his statement, or your notes for favorable facts* relating to the issues and assign a weight from 0 to 4 on the same basis as in step #4, *but to the right of each issue.*

7. *Total the scores* on each side of the issues.
8. *Now review his statement or your notes for impeachment* and assign a value of 1 to 4 to whatever you find, depending on your opinion of its likely effect on the trier of facts (judge or jury).
9. *Assign a value from 1 to 4 to the nature of the relationship between the witness and adverse party* (4 if it is the adverse party himself and a lesser number as the intimacy of the relationship decreases).
10. *Add the values in steps 8 and 9* and subtract from the left hand total obtained in step 7.
11. *Now compare* the remaining "unfavorable" total on the left with the "favorable" total on the right.

CONCLUSIONS TO DRAW

—If the witness scores a 4 to the left of any essential issue you or the opponent must prove to win or if the left hand total exceeds the right hand total by 3 or more times the number of issues, the witness will devastate you, and you should consider him a critical negative influence on case value.

—If the witness scores a 3 to the left of any essential issue or the left hand total exceeds the right hand total by 1½ to 3 times the number of issues, consider the witness a moderately negative influence on your case value.

—If the left hand total exceeds the right hand total by less than 1½ times the number of issues, the witness will probably do you negligible harm and you should not consider him in evaluating your case for settlement.

—Finally, if his score on the right hand side exceeds that on the left, consider him a slight positive influence on case value.

3

Interviewing The Disinterested
Witness And Others

TABLE OF CONTENTS

3

Interviewing The Disinterested Witness And Others

*"Imperfection is built into the nature of man so that
the first law of life is effort."*
John Bunyan

Section A.   INTERVIEWING THE DISINTERESTED WITNESS

THE OBJECTIVES OF A DISINTERESTED WITNESS INTERVIEW

This is a witness who possesses relevant facts about your case events and has no personal bias favoring either party, except that which his facts create. He carries a high credibility with those persons whom you wish to persuade, opposing counsel and party, third party (insurance company, indemnitor), judge and jury, such that, if his facts be controlling, he himself will control the outcome of settlement negotiations or trial.

> ACTION RULE: The disinterested witness, more than any other, including the client, is the key to winning or losing the liability issues of your case. As with any precious substance, he must be sought with zeal, mined with art, preserved with care, and protected against tampering.

Without an axe to grind or nest to feather, devoid of any allegiance to either side, this witness prefers not to become involved in your case to any extent. So he has either given his name as a witness and now regrets it, or has concealed his identity and is content to leave it that way.

Such is the profile of the average disinterested witness a lawyer encounters. It poses identification and location problems not usually experienced with friendly and unfriendly witnesses, whose bias prompts a high visibility.

Putting such problems aside for later treatment (See Chapter 4), the present concern is with the witness whose name and address are known to you. How do you go about interviewing him so as to maximize his benefit and minimize his detriment to your case?

Six Objectives To Reach

You should begin by knowing your objectives precisely in advance. Then you must utilize effective techniques during the interview itself to reach them. First the objectives:

1. *Interview the witness quickly and before your opponent does.* An emphasis was placed on holding speedy interviews with previous classes of witnesses already discussed. With them it was highly advisable. In the case of the disinterested witness, however, it is *absolutely imperative.* The usual reason for getting to him while his memory is vivid fits here, but beyond that is the witness' facility for disappearing—and your opponent's proficiency at confusing or influencing his facts.

2. *Obtain all relevant facts he knows about the events of your case, then determine whether, on balance, he is a benefit or detriment to your side.* The sum of the witness' facts usually fits him into one of four qualitative niches. He is either ... entirely favorable (as where all he saw was the other side drive into the rear of your stopped car) ... entirely unfavorable (your client drove into the rear of the adverse party's car and that is all he saw) ... more favorable than unfavorable (he saw adverse party drive into the rear of your car which had no brake lights working) ... more unfavorable than favorable (reverse last example).

   A decision on the witness' overall effect on your case is a must so you know whether to cope with his resistance to involvement or let it alone; whether to protect yourself against his disappearance or pray for it.

3. *If the witness is likely to benefit you, overcome his resistance to involvement by inducing a personal committment to the case.* Except for a meager minority who are willing to help because they are busybodies, or egoists, or they revere justice, most witnesses of this type enter an interview with the enthusiasm of a prisoner entering the death house. In their minds, there is no reason for helping you that outweighs the reasons why he should not (inconvenience, loss of income, nervous upset, lawyer "deception", etc.). Your task must be to supply the witness with positive reasons for helping the client that eclipse the negative ones ... endowing him with an incentive to participate that will last as long as your need of him.

4. *Induce a factual bias benefiting your client and mitigate as much as possible the unfavorable facts.* Instilling a desire to help you in a witness is not the same thing as eliciting facts from him that *will* help you, though the two are linked. Two witnesses rarely see the same event in the same way and never describe it identically. "After hearing sworn witnesses contradict each other concerning events both saw, I worry about history," a lawyer once remarked.

Having heard so often about sensory fallibility, most witnesses grudingly concede it in themselves and are amenable to influence up to a point. Your objective must be to find where that point is, i.e., what facts will he alter to conform to reason, logic, and other inconsistent or contradictory facts, and which will he stick to despite everything. Then you must alter what you can, ethically, by reference to the same guidelines of reason, logic, and other facts.

5. *Obtain leads to other facts, evidence, and witnesses you do not possess.* No matter what the value of his own testimony may be, a disinterested witness will sometimes be able to supply you with clues to the identity and whereabouts of that witness all lawyers dream about ... the conclusive witness. I know a lawyer who, while defending a grocery store robbery/homicide case, interviewed twelve patrons who had been on the scene before finding one who saw the murderer clearly and could exonerate the defendant. Only one of the twelve was identified in a police report. The lawyer learned of the others from successive interviews with each as he became known (the first gave clues leading to the second, the second for the third, etc.).

6. *If the witness' facts generally favor you, obtain sufficient personal data enabling you to locate him whenever necessary later on.* If it is sound advice to anticipate a friendly witness' disappearance during the pendancy of your case and prepare well in advance for it, it is a *commandment* in the case of the disinterested witness. Without any allegiance to your client, he will often sink into oblivion with never a thought for your distress.

WHEN, WHERE, AND HOW TO CONDUCT THE INTERVIEW

Whenever discussing interviewing techniques with lawyers, I am reminded of Descartes' observation:

Of all good things in the world the one that is most fairly distributed is good sense, because every man is so well satisfied with his own share.

Similarly, lawyers tend to be self-satisfied about their interviewing ability, thinking it a simple task—mere fact-gathering outside a courtroom setting. They sell it too short and pay for their error by invariably achieving too little from their interviews.

How Facts Are Influenced

A witness' sensory impressions, his recollections of them, even his communication of those recollections—all are shaped by a variety of influences. His logic is at work resisting a perception that defies common sense. His experience operates to cast doubt upon a recollection that contradicts prior perceptions. His self-esteem suppresses a communication which is likely to expose him to ridicule. Finally, a partisan affection, sympathy, or committment will soften a harsh fact and prompt him to explain, justify, and extenuate it.

Providing The Necessary Influences

A disinterested witness, by definition, has no partisan committment. You must give him one! Do his recalled facts that favor you strike him as illogical, unreasonable, or contrary to past experience? You must strengthen them, citing similar facts of others or simply arguing their validity. Do his recalled facts that injure you strike him as logical, reasonable, and consistent? You must weaken them when you can by citing contradictory or inconsistent facts of others, or arguing their invalidity.

Does the witness slough over facts that aid your cause because he thinks them insignificant? Show him their legal significance and emphasize them in his mind and statement. Does he exaggerate the importance of damaging facts? Set them in perspective and minimize them in his mind and statement.

Witness interviewing, then, is fact-gathering raised to an art form. The artists in our profession, lawyers who consistently win better settlements and judgments than average—with average cases—see it as a critical stage in developing a case to win. So must you. Here are several interviewing techniques to use with disinterested witnesses that have proven their worth time and time again.

CHECKLIST FOR SETTING UP
AND CONDUCTING THE INTERVIEW

1. *As soon as the client interview is done,* examine his checklist form and any other readily available source of facts (police report, official records, newspaper story, etc.) for names and addresses of disinterested witnesses who are likely to possess important facts bearing on some issue of your case. List the names in order of potential importance.

2. *After identifying such a disinterested witness,* phone him at his house or employment for an interview appointment as soon as possible. Explain your status and purpose; that you are investigating the case and *must* see and talk with him so that a settlement decision can be made intelligently. Delay the interview one hour longer than necessary and you risk losing the great advantage of priority to your opponent.

3. *If the witness refuses* or is reluctant to see you, tell him the interview is imperative; that you wish to make it as convenient for him as possible, so you will come to his house. Then say if he refuses to cooperate, you will have no choice but to take his testimony under court order *at your office and during the day.* If you do not bluster, but remain courteous throughout, he will surely relent, for the penalty of refusing an interview will seem to him worse than the annoyance from granting it.

4. *Interview the witness at his home* after work or on a weekend (find out during your phone conversation what time he eats, retires or plans some other activity, then schedule the interview to allow at least *two hours* with him). If you are unable to see him at his house within a reasonable period of time, try to persuade him to come to your office. Emphasize how vital he is to the case and the need for haste. A witness will sometimes be so flattered by your attention that he will deal generously with you.

5. *When interviewing at his home, ask if the two of you can go to a room away from the rest of the family* where you can talk alone. Privacy is essential for two reasons: 1) The physical and vocal presence of Junior, Sis, and Mom (often all three) is distracting; it interferes with the flow of questions and answers and the desired empathy between you; and 2) The effect of an audience on a witness is the same as it is on an actor ... both tend to emote and grandstand. He is conscious of his "image," and is much less ready to admit he may be wrong on some fact or recollection.

6. *Ask the witness to narrate events* he witnessed while you make notes of

relevant facts. Underline those facts which have a marked bearing on a case issue. Then question him closely about the underlined material while you test the following: 1) The consistency of his story (i.e., Do details change from one time to the next?); 2) The degree of certainty with which he holds and relates the facts (i.e., Does he hesitate or look evasive, his manner suggesting doubt? Do his words suggest it? . . . "I think it happened this way" . . . "It seems to me that he said . . ."); 3) Whether his facts are general and undiscriminating ("There was a stop sign at the corner but I don't remember much about it.") or detailed and precise ("It was two feet from the curb and a foot from the cross-walk.")

7. *Whenever the witness evinces uncertainty* about favorable facts and you obtained the same facts from another source (client or friendly witness interview, official reports, personal investigation, etc.), identify the source to him and reinforce the facts in his mind. When his uncertainty relates to unfavorable facts and you obtained conflicting facts from another source, identify the source and other facts. Seek an admission from the witness that he may be mistaken.

8. *Write a memorandum statement* of the witness' facts using the writing techniques and authentication presented in Chapter 5. Have him sign or initial each page and give him a copy bearing your name, address, and phone number. *Ask him to read his statement privately before discussing the case with the lawyer or representative of the adverse party.* Explain that he will be less likely to make an inconsistent or contradictory statement if he does.

9. *If you have time, complete a witness interview form* (See Chapter 2) in his presence. It is a further check on his facts, is more orderly and complete than his statement and is insurance against the statement being lost. If you do not have time to fill out the entire form, be sure to complete Section A, which asks for personal information to help you trace the witness if he disappears.

10. *If the witness is favorable,* for your case, find out if he has present plans to move and, if so, where, and when. Also ask him about his health. If he is aged or infirm, make prominent note of it on your file jacket so that his deposition will be taken if settlement negotiations fail and suit is filed.

11. *If your case involves a spatial event* (traffic accident, crime, trespass, or nuisance) have him diagram whatever he witnessed, then sign or initial the diagram. If a picture is worth a thousand words, a diagram is worth ten thousand because it bears the personal imprint of the diagrammer.

12. *If the witness denies seeing anything of value* and sticks to the denial

under your questioning, take his statement anyway and quote the denial. How often has such a know-nothing witness miraculously discovered a recollection at some later date? The experience of every lawyer is peppered with such surprises. Have his written disclaimer and he is impeached. Fail to have it and you may be duped.

13. *Interview a witness by phone only when no other interview can be obtained.* It is like reeling in a catfish when you are fishing for pike. Something is better than nothing. That small something could grow much larger if, for example, you ask him on the witness stand, "Didn't you tell me on the phone that you never saw the accident at all?" . . . and he answers, "Yes."

COAXING VALUABLE COMMITMENTS FROM THE WITNESS

Lawyers, like other people, think too much in stereotypes. "Because he is a veteran lawyer he must be skilled; because he is a young lawyer he must be artless; because defendant is a corporation the settlement value must be greater; because this juror is young and Italian he must be pro-plaintiff; because that juror is old and retired he must be pro-defendant."

Generalizations of this type are dangerous because experience so often refutes them.

Another stereotype to avoid is this one . . . because he is a disinterested witness he must have no interest in the outcome of your case. Avoid it not because it is untrue in theory *but because you can make it untrue in practice by instilling an interest . . . that benefits your case.*

Coping With Witness Indifference By Personalization

It is true that lacking the kind of relationship with a party that spurs a friendly or unfriendly witness to a partisan stance, a disinterested witness does not much care who wins or loses and would rather not get involved at all.

> **ACTION RULE: At the outset of the interview, seek to create a favorable bias in the witness by personalizing your client and his cause. Build a verbal image so that the witness is forced to think of him as a flesh and blood being who may be helped or hurt by what the witness says or does.**

Describe your client and his family in detail, as though answering the question, "Who is he and what is he like?" Speak of him as if he were a friend as well as a client. ("Mr. Jones, I represent Dan Smith who was one of the drivers involved in the accident you know about. Dan's a young man, 26, and big . . . about 6 feet 2 I'd say. He and his wife, Sue, have three children, all boys. They live on the south side of town in a small bungalow they own . . . together with a bank, of course. Dan's a hard-working guy with a good driving record. This was his first accident, I understand, and no arrests.")

Then describe the client's injury and/or damages if he is the claimant or the demands made of him if he is the defendant, and explain the nature of the recovery you seek to obtain for the client (claimant) or the nature of the jeopardy you are defending him from (defendant).

I'm trying to get a settlement from the other driver's insurance company that will put Dan back on his feet again; pay his bills, pay his lost wages, protect him against any future disability and compensate him in a small way for the pain and trouble he's had.

Or . . .

I'm trying to protect Dan and Sue against losing their home and everything they've worked so hard to get. The other driver's demanding much more than their insurance coverage. Than, too, there's Dan's insurance premiums. If he loses this case he'll be paying much higher premiums for years, no matter what the other man gets.

Then ask the witness point blank to help you "in any way he can" so that you can help your client.

It is vital that you convey absolute sincerity and earnestness in your description of the client. That means (unless you are a consummate actor) telling only truth about him. If he is a drunken slob who beats his wife and gets stoned every other day, you need not mention it. But do not portray him as a loving husband of good habits.

The reward of an induced witness bias favorable to your client is an end to indifference and a beginning of a desire to help. The witness is now ready and willing to cooperate with you, to be interviewed at length and respond truthfully; ready to give you a written statement, to be open-minded (amendable to fact persuasion) and to appear for pre-trial discovery and trial testimony if necessary.

Bias Is No Substitute For Facts

With all its charm and value, a good bias is no cure for bad facts. (No silk purse can be made from a sow's ear.) If a witness' facts are entirely adverse to you, he is convinced of their accuracy and cannot be shaken, then no amount of bias building will make an asset of him.

But what about making a pigskin purse? Even the most antagonistic witness can usually be left better than you find him. He may not renounce his damaging facts but he is likely to soften them. "He was racing down the road like a hot rodder" becomes . . . "He was driving a bit fast." "There's no doubt it was him holding the gun" becomes . . . "I think it was him holding the gun." The difference amounts to winning or losing.

WHEN AND HOW MUCH TO PAY THE WITNESS

From time to time an important disinterested witness will appear whom you will be unable to interview at his house, either because you cannot get there within a reasonable time or because he is unwilling to receive you there. You are left with three choices; do without his interview, interview him by phone, or persuade him to come to your office and interview him there.

The third option is obviously the one to choose. The first is no choice at all, while the second is always a last resort, to be seized only when no hope of an in-person interview exists.

Why Money Is Often The Necessary Persuasion

Persuading the witness to come to you is easier decided upon than done. He will not come at night for personal reasons and will not come during the day for economic reasons. A friendly witness will make such sacrifices on request. A disinterested witness normally will not. You must remove the element of sacrifice to get him to come. Agree to pay him for a daytime office interview, but only as much as will spare him a loss, not earn him a profit.

> **ACTION RULE: Whenever a potentially important disinterested witness can only be interviewed at your office within a reasonable time and refuses to come there for economic reasons (lost wages, transportation expense,**

baby-sitting cost, etc.) promise to reimburse him in full for whatever loss and/or cost is incurred. Find out over the phone what sums are involved and ask him to bring records or receipts to verify any wage item. At the end of the interview pay the agreed sum whether the witness turned out to be helpful or hurtful to your case. Then be sure to prepare and have him sign a receipt stating the amount paid and items it covered.

Antipathy to paying a non-expert witness any money any time is a foolish scruple because it fails to distinguish between a reimbursement and a reward. Pay reasonable interview expenses and no opponent will penalize you during settlement negotiations—because no judge or jury will do it during trial.

An Attack On A "Paid Witness" That Backfired

Once in a while, a lawyer in court will attempt to show corruption in the act of reimbursing a witness. But it rarely comes off and sometimes wounds the lawyer instead.

Bill Roberts was the witness, a man in his sixties who, stolidly but effectively, gave important testimony for the plaintiff in a breach of contract case. Under cross-examination, he admitted accepting $20 from plaintiff's counsel following his interview in the latter's office. Defense counsel seized on this with relish.

He paid you that because you told him what he wanted to hear, isn't that a fact?
No, sir.
Did you know you would get $20 before you began talking to him about this case?
Before the interview. Yes, sir.
So the $20 was your payment for telling a good story, isn't that true?
No, sir.
Then what was it for, (the lawyer shouted).
My wife, Cora, was paralyzed at home and had to have all-the-time attention. I paid $20 to hire a nurse for the afternoon so I could get to his office.

Unwilling to concede defeat, the lawyer pursued the subject with disastrous results . . . .

How much are you getting to come to court to testify?
Nothing.
Oh, said the lawyer, looking at the jury significantly, you mean you had to have $20 to go to an attorney's office but nothing to come to this court. How do you explain that?
My Cora's dead now. She don't need any more nursing now.

Roberts' eyes began tearing. So did the eyes of the judge, jury and defense counsel (the last for a different reason). Verdict was for plaintiff. Roberts was the reason, the jurors said later. As one of them put it, "Such a loyal and loving man, he had to be telling the entire truth."

Why Paying More Than Expenses Is Fatal

There is indeed a fine line between virtue and vice. While paying a witness expenses seems reasonable, paying him $1 more than expenses seems a bribe. Had the lawyer paid Bill Roberts more than it cost to care for Cora that afternoon, the jury's reaction to him, the lawyer and the case, might have been different.

> **ACTION RULE:** If a witness demands a sum in excess of his loss and expense as a condition of his coming to your office for interview, refuse him. Tell him you will pay in full whatever he is out by coming, but that your rules of ethics prohibit more (as they do). Never promise to pay a witness more as an enticement, then refuse it afterwards, for you will end up paying more in terms of his vengeful trial testimony.

There is an old adage you should keep in mind: "The cost of buying up a witness is selling out your case."

EVALUATING THE DISINTERESTED WITNESS

To know the settlement value of your case, you must know its trial value, and to know its trial value you must first evaluate all witnesses; friendly, unfriendly, disinterested, and client alike. What is the content of their testimony? How does it relate to the issues? What will it tend to prove or disprove? To what degree? Will their personalities and manner of testifying have a positive, negative, or neutral effect on judge or jury?

"Balance Sheet" For The Disinterested Witness

1. *Complete a witness evaluation form* (Figure 1-3), reflecting the witness' appearance, personality, intelligence, etc., as soon as possible after his interview.
2. *List the essential issues* of your case in column form in the center of a page of paper.
3. *Review the witness' written statement* (or your notes if no statement was

obtained or a court reporter was present) for *unfavorable* facts relating to each listed issue.

4. *Assign a numerical weight* from 0 to 4 to the left of each issue on the page according to the tendency of his unfavorable facts to prove or disprove it.

5. *Review the witness statement or your notes for favorable facts* relating to the listed issues and assign a weight from 0 to 4 *to the right of each issue.*

6. *Total the scores* on each side of the issues column.

7. *Assign a weight* from 0 to 4 representing your opinion of the witness' superficial qualities as shown by his evaluation form. Now add this number *to whichever total score is larger.* The value of his personality, intelligence, appearance, and manner will be greatest for the party his facts favor.

8. *Only if the total score on the left side exceeds that on the right,* review his statement or your notes for impeachment and assign a value from 1 to 4 to whatever you find, depending on your opinion of its likely effect on the trier of facts (judge or jury). Subtract this number from the left-hand score.

9. *Now compare* the remaining "unfavorable" total on the left with the "favorable" total on the right.

Conclusions You Should Draw: The Disinterested Witness

—If he scores a 4 to the left or right of any essential issue, or if either side exceeds the other by 3 or more times the number of issues, he will be a strong witness for (right) or against (left) you.

—If one side exceeds the other by 1½ to 3 times the number of issues, he will be a moderately effective witness for or against you.

—If one side exceeds the other by less than 1½ times the number of issues, the witness will have little effect. You should not consider him in evaluating your settlement value.

Section B.   INTERVIEWING THE POLICE OR GOVERNMENTAL WITNESS

HOW TO ARRANGE AND CONDUCT THE INTERVIEW

I remember asking a detective sergeant what he does when a defense lawyer attempts to interview him about a pending case:

I Snarl!

But what if he persists?
I tell him I have something to do.
And if he waits?
Then I'll sit down and talk to him. I don't want to get him sore.

This policeman is a member of a large metropolitan force, but his attitude typifies that of policemen everywhere—avoid an interview at some, but not all cost, but do not make the lawyer angry with you.

The anecdote suggests the extent you must go to interview every governmental witness (police, fire marshal, building inspector, etc.) who has played a significant investigative role in your case. Official reports of agencies involved, and information from your client and other witnesses tell you who they are. The rest is up to you and depends on boldness, persistence, and an effective interviewing technique.

Why The Interview Is Vital . . . Action Example

A lawyer acquaintance of mine told me about this case, which he lost because he neglected to interview the investigating officer. It was an automobile negligence case and he represented plaintiff, a young married man who was driving his employer's car at the time of the accident. He had been hired as a salesman a short time before and was still on probation when the collision occurred.

The case looked like a sure winner for plaintiff. The police report placed the center of debris on plaintiff's side of the yellow center line, confirming his story that defendant's car was on the wrong side of the road. A big winner, moreover, because plaintiff sustained fractures to his left arm, left ribs, and a punctured lung. He was hospitalized three weeks and off work nine months. Defendant was covered by a hundred thousand dollar policy. *A settlement offer of twelve thousand dollars was made and rejected before trial.*

There was only one thing about the case that should have disturbed plaintiff's lawyer just a little, that defendant had claimed plaintiff had been drinking; that the smell of liquor was all about him and strong in the car. But plaintiff denied it and there was nothing in the police report to corroborate the claim (questions regarding drinking were left blank) so the lawyer remained confident until the end, which came abruptly at the trial, during the following cross-examination dialogue between defense counsel and the police officer.

Isn't it a fact, officer, that Mr. Stull (plaintiff) had been drinking a short time before this accident?

Yes, sir.

What was he drinking?

Scotch and water.

How do you know that?

He told me.

Did plaintiff tell you anything else about his drinking?

He said he had 2 shots of scotch about a half hour before the accident.

Do you have an opinion about his drinking?

I think he had a good deal to drink. The smell was very strong.

Anticipating re-direct, defense counsel drove home the final nail and left my friend with nothing to cling to.

Tell me, officer, why didn't you put this information about Stull's drinking into your report?

I should have, but I felt sorry for him. He asked me not to report it. He said he'd just started to work for this company and would be fired if they found out.

Not surprisingly, the jury returned a defense verdict. Instead of banking a substantial fee, my friend had to pay substantial expenses. If he had only interviewed the officer early in the case, he would have discovered his jeopardy and settled, *for at the time the $12,000 was offered the defense had not interviewed him either.*

> **ACTION RULE: Significant facts are often omitted, garbled, or misrepresented in official reports of criminal, accident, and other governmental investigations. So whenever such an investigation is prominent in your case, interview the principal investigators personally and promptly.**

CHECKLIST FOR INTERVIEWING POLICE AND GOVERNMENTAL WITNESSES

1. *Interview the witness personally* at his office or station without prior notice or appointment. If he is a police or fireman, find out his duty hours first, then see him at his station a short time before or immediately after his shift.

2. *Identify yourself and client* to the witness and tell him you are investigating the case "to determine whether to settle it or not." You will find police witnesses much more congenial once they think you will settle the accident case or plead your client guilty to something, because they hope to escape a court appearance (police officers have an unshakeable conviction that a summons to court always comes on a day off).

3. *Adopt a manner of calm confidence* as though you fully expect the witness to cooperate and will not tolerate a refusal. An intrepid demeanor is vital to a successful interview with these witnesses, who can be some of the most arrogant, yet fear-ridden, members of society (Who will get the promotion? What political influences are working against him? Will moonlighting be abolished? Will he be transferred to a worse beat? Will this lawyer make trouble for him?).

4. *If an official report was made by the witness, get a copy* beforehand and review it as you interview him. Ask these questions concerning it:
   —Does he recall any facts not stated in the report?
   —Are all facts stated in the report accurate, according to his notes, memory and subsequent investigation?
   —Will he resolve any ambiguity or apparent conflict in facts stated in the report?

5. *Ask the witness if he obtained an oral or written statement* from anyone involved in the case (especially your client, adverse party and agents of either). If a statement was orally given, ask if he made notes of what was said at the time or merely recalls it from memory. Ask the witness to read over his notes before quoting. If written statements were taken, ask for a copy of each and offer to pay for them (nearly all police and other agencies have copying equipment). Should he refuse you a copy, gently but firmly insist, pointing to the alternative of your applying to court for a turnover order or using a discovery tool.

6. *Ask the witness if any photographs, measurements, and/or diagrams were made* by himself or another agency investigator. If so, ask that copies be made at your expense. Should he refuse you copies, ask to see the originals and copy the measurements and diagrams yourself.

7. *Whenever you discover an error in the official report* (your client is identified as driver of the speeding car who caused the collision when in fact he drove the other car) immediately call it to the attention of the witness and *demand* that it be corrected. The longer you delay correction the more difficult it becomes as the preparer's memory dims, his notes are misplaced or he, himself, leaves for another job at a distant place.

8. *If the witness balks at discussing the case with you,* tell him that unless he cooperates for a few minutes you will have to take his deposition at a place and time of your choosing.

9. *Finally, should the witness flatly refuse to discuss the case with you,* make a note of his refusal verbatim and preserve it. If the case goes to trial it will be useful material upon which to cross-examine him, suggesting an unreasonable bias against you and client and a desire to suppress facts. If you learn (as you will sometimes) that your opponent advised the witness not to discuss the case with you, record this fact too.

It contributes an added settlement pressure since the lawyer's conduct is a borderline violation of Disciplinary Rule 7-109 (A) of the Code of Professional Responsibility.

Obtaining Leads To Other Facts And Witnesses

The saying that "An opportunity always looks bigger going than coming," is as true in law as in life. How many times have you failed to ask a question of a witness in the courtroom and later convinced yourself the answer would have made the difference, though the question seemed innocuous at the time? How often have you declined a case as hopeless, later to be persuaded you could have won it?

But the largest waste lies not in the direction of ignored opportunities, but rather in that there are so many unseen opportunities. Chances of victory that appear . . . and pass by . . . because they are not recognized.

One such opportunity that few lawyers recognize involves police and other governmental witnesses. It is the chance during their interview to snare leads to vital facts and witnesses previously unknown. These witnesses are usually trained investigators with noses and eyes for scents and signs, clues to the identity and whereabouts of a hidden witness, the location of documents and needed exhibits and the possibility that the simple explanation of the accident or crime may not be the right one.

> ACTION RULE: Ask for more than facts during an interview with a police or other governmental witness. Ask for his opinions, suppositions, even downright guesses regarding the existence and whereabouts of other facts and witnesses important to your case. And ask him to check with any colleague who may have worked on your case for similar responses.

EXAMPLES OF LEADS THAT CAN BE OBTAINED

A tow truck operator is called to every crash scene in America where a car has been disabled to remove it from the road. It is customary for him to sweep crash debris off the pavement, so that he becomes a potential witness to the point of impact.

Police reports commonly do not identify the tow truck operator who came to the scene, but the odds are good that the investigating police officer knows him. And if he does not know who he is, he can find out, for it is the practice of most police departments to maintain a list of "approved" towing companies and limit calls to these in some prescribed order. Ask the officer involved in your case to check the department log book and tow truck list for the name of the operator who was called. If this is fruitless, then ask him to describe the truck and operator. Using the yellow pages, call all operators within the near vicinity of the accident scene and match the descriptions. You will be pleased with the frequent success of this approach.

Here is a list of several other leads that can contribute to your results:

From A Policeman In An Auto Negligence Case:

—*Description of ambulance vehicle and driver* that removed accident victim from scene to the hospital and may have overheard impeaching utterances . . . witness' opinion of who it was.

—*Witness' opinion about the garage(s) or lot(s)* where the disabled vehicles were towed from the scene, based on his knowledge of past practices.

—*His speculation regarding the identity of eyewitnesses* to the case events, whose names were not obtained the scene for various reasons. Based upon everything he can recall or was told about them. (e.g., Appear to be passers-by or neighborhood residents? Anything distinctive in their dress? Mailman's uniform, laborer's clothes, gas station attendant, etc.?)

—*His knowledge or surmise whether another or other police officers worked on your case.* No indication of this will usually appear on public reports. If asked, the witness will often name the other officers or state his belief that they were involved. In either event, you may assume they possess facts important to you and should interview them also.

—*His knowledge or assumptions regarding police events subsequent to your client's arrest,* i.e., lineups not involving client; transport of exhibits to crime lab for analysis; another arrest for same offense.

—*His knowledge (fact or rumor) about your client's criminal record* of past arrests and convictions.

—*His opinion of your client's guilt.* (It is surprising how candid police officers are . . . lower echelons only . . . in answering the question, "From what you know of the case, officer, do you think my client's guilty?" and supporting the opinion with reasons. In a fair number of cases the answer is, "I'm not sure. There's evidence against him, but . . . well, he sure acts and speaks like he's telling the truth.") Any opinion other than "He's guilty as Hell" has to be uplifting, for it means the presence of "reasonable doubt."

From A Zoning Inspector In A Municipal Zoning Case:

—*His knowledge or opinion about other land uses* similar to yours which were allowed in the same locale. His opinion about past interpretations of zoning code sections applicable to your case.

From A Municipal Building Inspector In A Construction Contract Case:

—*His opinions about the existence of defects* in the structure, the reasonable cost of repairing them and artisans you should hire for same.

From A Coroner Or Deputy In Wrongful Death And Homicide Cases:

—*His opinion ruling out any causal agent of death but the accident event . . .* or his opinion that another or other medical conditions not connected with client's actions contributed to death.

Section C.   INTERVIEWING THE MEDICAL AND OTHER EXPERT WITNESS

WHY, WHERE AND HOW TO CONDUCT THE INTERVIEW

By definition, an expert witness is a person who, by virtue of his education, experience and training, is entitled to express an opinion in court on the subject of his expertise. He is most commonly a physician, but is often a dentist (personal injury tort case), traffic engineer (auto negligence case), real estate appraiser (condemnation or tort or contract case involving land), economist (injury case involving disability or death) or criminal identification specialist (fingerprint, ballistics, chemical and spectroscope).

Though he generally pursues his specialty as a profession, it is no prerequisite; his skill, training and experience are what count. A recent case involved a plaintiff who fractured his hip while hopping on a pogo stick (he was jabbed in the ribs by a playful friend while in mid-hop). A fifteen-year-old boy qualified as an expert witness to offer opinions about the art and hazards of pogo sticking.

Why You Need An Expert And Need To Be Sure Of His Opinions

Whenever your case involves an important element beyond the under-standing and experience of the public as a whole (diagnosis and prognosis of a hip fracture, reasonable market value of land, pogo stick hopping, etc.) you need an expert witness. You need him because he adds value to your case; he adds value by reason of his expertise. He can better persuade your opponent, a jury, and judge to accept your claims.

You will often find an expert deeply involved in your case by the time you enter it (e.g., your client's treating physician or real estate broker). Others you must choose yourself.

Here is the vital information you must obtain before you can decide intelligently the dimension of his contribution to case value.

Checklist Of Things To Learn From The Expert

1. Learn all the opinions he has relevant to any case issue.
2. Determine whether the opinions are final or provisional. If provisional, learn when he is likely to have final opinions.
3. Determine whether any opinion is conditional and, if so, learn the nature of the condition.
4. Appraise the strength of his opinions (is he positive, reasonably sure, or uncertain).
5. Determine the bases of the opinions (scientifically demonstrable, probable, or possible).
6. Learn the facts underlying the opinions and make certain all are correct (Was your client in a rear-end collision or was it a side-swipe?). Change any erroneous facts and ask how the changes affect his opinions.
7. Make the expert explain any opinion you do not clearly understand. If it is too obscure for you it will be obscure to others and therefore useless.
8. Get a committment from him that he will testify in court if necessary and will state the same opinions there. Making it clear to him at the interview that he may be required to testify at trial and be subjected to cross-examination provides you some assurance that the opinions he espouses today will be the same that he expresses tomorrow.
9. Obtain a summary of his qualifications, i.e., the specialized education, training, research and experience qualifying him as an expert. Then ask how much of his qualifications relates to the specifics of your case. (How many hip fractures has he handled? What percentage of his appraisals has been of commercial properties?) Many expert witnesses have qualification resumes already prepared. Be sure to ask for one.
10. Learn the extent of his experience testifying in court. Given the same

qualifications, an experienced witness contributes more value to your case than an inexperienced one and should be given added weight when determining your settlement level. He has learned the importance of "stage presence" in the courtroom, exhibiting perfect certitude in the face of a hostile cross-examiner.

Why A Written Report Is Not An Adequate Substitute

Many lawyers are content to obtain information from a written report submitted by the expert and forego the interview, thinking to save their time and his fee. It is a foolish economy, akin to boarding up the bathroom because the toilet leaks.

By all means get his written report first, but always interview him after.

"Obscurism" among experts is not confined just to the fabled poor penmanship of the doctor. They are not specialists in English composition. Their reports are often ambiguous and confusing, sometimes gravely misleading and downright inaccurate.

Two Examples of Expert Witness Reports That Led To Bad Settlements

A case that stirred some currents in a midwest city involved a fourteen-year-old bicyclist who lost a joust with a Buick and suffered a bad fracture of his left leg. Liability was clear and insurance coverage heavy. The only significant question affecting settlement value was the extent of the boy's future disability.

His treating orthopedist, an eminent local specialist, wrote a lengthy closing report to claimant's lawyer which concluded with the following prognosis:

In my opinion, open reduction surgery accomplished all objectives and the patient's post-operative course has been normal. Further progress will be experienced and the present disability, consisting of a left foot drop caused by nerve involvement, will gradually improve until is stabilized.

Thinking that "stabilized" in this context referred to the foot, counsel proceeded to settle his case on the basis of no permanent injury. Sometime later the boy's father came storming into the lawyer's office and accused him of "selling them out." It seems the doctor had just told him his son would probably have a permanent foot drop.

When the lawyer accused the orthopedist of misrepresenting the situation in his report, the latter indignantly replied that he had described the future course precisely right; that the disability would improve to a point and then remain steady thereafter.

The Case Of The Missing Tunnel

Then there was the condemnation case in which a state proposed eliminating a railroad crossing by constructing a roadway overpass. Since the roadway bisected the owner's grain field, the central factor affecting damages was access . . . or lack of it. The approach ramp was to be elevated across the owner's frontage and bordered with guard rails.

Counsel hired an experienced real estate appraiser to investigate the question and report his opinion of damages. The report read, in part, as follows:

Based on evidence that the State will provide access to the 8.3 acre parcel via a tunnel through the ramp, it is my opinion that damage to the residue amounts to $16,000.

The report went on to an elaborate calculation explaining the figure. It was an impressive piece of work, the expert's credentials were impeccable and the case was settled on the basis of the opinion.

Six months later the construction work was complete and there was no tunnel. Inquiry by the lawyer of the State disclosed that it had never been planned. When the expert was confronted he revealed his "evidence." He had discussed the case with the State's appraiser who told him that tunnels were customarily provided in such instances and he . . . the State's man . . . had no doubt it would be installed here too.

Of course, the lawyer advised his client he had a case against the expert stemming from the latter's negligence. But by this time the owner was convinced he had a case against his lawyer too and had retained new counsel to pursue it.

ACTION RULE: Interview the expert witness in his office whenever you can arrange it, to be sure that all records, notes, charts, drawings, computations, instruments and other materials used in forming his opinions are accessible to you. Make an appointment and reserve all the time you need.

Whatever you save in personal inconvenience by bringing the expert to you, you will lose two-fold in the extra fee you pay him and the inadequacy of his presentation.

> **REMEMBER:** The purpose of your interview is not to review the expert's opinions but to test them; not so much to learn what they are as to learn if they are accurate, coherent, understandable and reasonable. If they are all these things to you, they are likely to be so to your opponent, making the task of settling at or near your terms easier.

Determining How Much To Pay
For The Interview

Few subjects cause greater dissension between lawyers and their expert witnesses than money. I saw a case destroyed by the indifferent testimony of a doctor who resented the refusal of his reasonable fee demand; and another case lost when plaintiff's counsel fired his traffic engineer over a fee dispute on the eve of trial and the judge refused a continuance.

Another type of money problem leading to diminished settlement and trial results stems from a different cause ... not from dissension but agreement. The lawyers promise or pay exorbitant fees to their experts only to find the latter's opinions met with a skepticism proportioned to the excess. Compensation becomes bribery when reasonableness is missing.

> **ACTION RULE:** Pay a fee to your expert for interviewing him. Always arrange the amount of it in advance, remembering that it is his time and not his opinions you are buying. Never agree to pay more than his standard charge to others for equivalent time. If he says he has no standard charge, ask what he would charge your client for an office visit merely to answer questions, then fix the fee accordingly, pointing out that it is the client's money you spend (true even if your fee is contingent). Pay him by office check promptly on submission of his bill and attach the cancelled check to your file jacket for future reference and display.

"You get what you pay for" is a familiar cliche, familiar because often used, and often used because it's true. Even if your expert offers not to charge you for the interview, do not accept. Chances are he will not prepare for your coming, will not concentrate while you are there, will short you on time and short change you on value.

"I won't treat relatives," a doctor friend once told me only half facetiously. "I can't charge a fee and I see them so hastily, I'm afraid I'll kill them with a wrong diagnosis."

Agree on the amount of the fee when you call for an interview appointment in order to remove the chance of disagreement at the interview itself. Should he demand more than his standard time charge, explain the potential damage to your case from paying it. Tell him your opponent will surely ask about the fee and if it is excessive over the norm, make much of that fact, implying that his opinions were influenced by the size of the fee.

Say that you know the expert's opinions would never be dollar-oriented, but that your opponent and his client will believe it and . . . what is worse . . . a jury and judge may believe it too.

This argument is effective because most experts understand about cross-examination and witness credibility and vanity is almost as strong a goad as greed.

WHY YOU SHOULD INTERVIEW YOUR OPPONENT'S EXPERTS . . . HOW TO DO IT

Many lawyers seem to feel there is something sinful about contacting another's expert witness . . . that talking is tampering, like prying open his file drawer and rifling his papers. It is a remnant of the sporting theory of advocacy that has resisted the discovery movement of recent times, which decrees that full disclosure of matters of relevance is to be preferred over secrecy.

There are the same reasons for interviewing an adverse expert as for interviewing an adverse party . . . to learn what he will say relative to your case and obtain bases for impeaching him—and one important restriction less. The Code of Professional Responsibility bars communication with a party known to be represented by counsel (Disciplinary Rule 7-104 (A)(1)). No such rule applies to the adverse party's expert.

Here are some techniques that will help you see and interview him.

Checklist Of Techniques For Interviewing An Adverse Expert

—*As soon as you learn the identity of an adverse expert* (from adverse party interview, opponent or your investigation) attempt to interview him personally at his office, at a time when he is sure to be in and without prior notice. You can easily learn his schedule from his secretary by phone without revealing your purpose.

—*Identify yourself as counsel for the other party* and tell him you are investigating the case to learn all possible facts and opinions bearing on it. Explain that you come to him to save him time, money and inconvenience; that if you do not obtain his information now, you may have to take his deposition at your office and seriously disrupt his schedule (Federal Rule of Civil Procedure #26 and State Rule counterparts permit a deposition of an adverse expert whom the opponent intends calling as a witness if the case is tried).

—*Offer to pay for his time based on his standard fee* to patients for consultation without treatment and promise to take but 15 minutes.

—*If his secretary intercepts you,* send the above explanation and offer to him through her . . . and wait! The expert will have difficulty refusing to speak with you, for three reasons: 1) He probably earns substantial fees from lawyers and will not want to risk losing a prospective client; 2) He will be impressed that you come to him in person and will take pains not to offend you; 3) He dislikes depositions because they are inconvenient, impair his earnings, and subject him to vigorous inquisition.

—*If he is a doctor or dentist,* tell him you need his information to determine whether to make an out-of-court settlement and, if so, on what terms. (It is a rare doctor or dentist who welcomes testifying in court. Most earn far more money spending comparable time in their offices and hospitals and are treated with reverence besides.

—*Ask the expert for his facts and conclusions* (opinions) generally as they relate to your case. You will often have a few brief minutes only before he returns to his work or changes his mind about talking with you, so once he begins discussing the case interrupt sparingly and only with a question.

—*Do not argue, show skepticism or cross-examine him.* Do not mention facts, findings or opinions which are contrary to his. The surest way to be disagreeable to him is to disagree.

—*If the expert is the adverse party's treating doctor* and, thus, is barred by the doctor/patient privilege from discussing the substance of his work, ask for the dates of his office visits and treatments. This information is helpful in verifying or refuting the adverse party's claims and is not covered by the privilege shield.

—*Make careful note of his appearance, manner, apparent intelligence and know-how,* articulateness and other factors covered in the Witness Evaluation Form (Figure 1-3). Then complete such a form as soon as possible after returning to your office.

—*Ask him for a brief summary of his education,* training, and experience for use in further evaluating him as a witness.

—*If, despite everything, the expert refuses to speak with you,* make note of the date, time and circumstances of the refusal for future courtroom reference should a trial occur.

Why Not Succeeding Is Better Than Not Trying

These techniques are by no means foolproof. Experience has shown on an average only a 50 percent chance of a successful interview wherein the expert discloses facts and opinions . . . slightly higher among suburban and rural experts and slightly lower among those in cities. But what advantage when you succeed!

You obtain key opposition information more accurately and far faster than if you wait for your opponent to reveal it . . . if he ever does. In states without liberal discovery provisions, he is under no duty to reveal it until trial. Even where Rule #26 operates, you can discover it only if your opponent names the expert as a prospective trial witness.

True, many federal and state courts have adopted supplementary rules requiring the exchange of experts' information. But this normally does not take place until the pre-trial conference and often consists of written reports from which damaging information has been withheld.

Even an interview that is refused returns a reward. Should settlement efforts fail and the case be tried, elicit an admission from the expert during cross-examination that he refused to discuss the case with you.

> REMEMBER: Any fact showing partisanship in an expert witness detracts from his professional image in a jury's eyes and weakens the impact of his testimony.

EVALUATING THE EXPERT WITNESS TO DETERMINE CASE SETTLEMENT VALUE

The task of weighing the impact of an expert witness on your case value is made easier by using a numerical weighting method similar to that used for disinterested witnesses earlier. Once a point total is found for him, whether he is your expert or your opponent's, a reasonably accurate prediction can then be made concerning his probable effect on case outcome. Considered in conjunction with other witness evaluations and factors explored in Chapter 7, you can then make an intelligent determination of the level at which your civil or criminal case should be settled.

Checklist For Evaluating Expert Witnesses

1. *Complete a Witness Evaluation Form* if it has not already been done.
2. *If he is an expert in the area of liability* (civil fault: traffic engineer, physicist, metallurgist, etc.) (criminal guilt: chemist, finger print or handwriting expert, etc.) write down in a column the essential issues or elements of your case (*for negligence case*; "negligence," "proximate cause of," "contributory negligence," "proximate cause of"—for larceny case; "purposeful taking," "another's property," "intent to permanently deprive of").
   a. Review the expert's facts, findings and opinions from your notes of his interview and mentally group them alongside the appropriate issues or elements.
   b. Assign a number from 1 to 4 opposite the affected issue(s) or element(s) according to the degree to which his facts, findings and opinions favor or injure your position, i.e., tend to prove or disprove the related issue. "1" signifies only a slight tendency; "2" a moderate tendency; "3" a strong; and "4" a conclusive probative tendency. If *injury results to your position, assign a minus number, weighted as above.*
   c. Now assign a number from 1 to 4 opposite the same issue(s) or element(s) as in the prior step, representing your appraisal of his Witness Evaluation Form. "1" signifies a poor overall personal profile likely to produce a negative reaction from a judge or jury, "2" a fair profile (ambivalent reaction), "3" a good profile (positive reaction), and "4" an outstanding profile (strongly positive reaction) from judge and jury. *Again, assign a minus number if the expert is adverse to you.*
   d. Add the two numbers together for each affected issue or element.
3. *If the witness is an expert in the area of civil damages* (doctor, dentist, auto body repairman, real estate appraiser) assume that a plaintiff's verdict is rendered on liability issues.
   a. Review the expert's facts, findings and opinions from your notes of his interview.
   b. Assign a number from 0 to 4 according to your judgment whether his facts, findings and opinions tend to support no damages ("0"), damages less than average for plaintiff's claims ("1"), average damages for his claims ("2"), above average damages ("3"), and top-dollar damages ("4").

Note: Refer to Chapter 7 for aid in determining the "average" damages expectable according to the claims of plaintiff in your case.

c. Now add a number from 1 to 4 to the number in the prior step representing your appraisal of the expert's Witness Evaluation Form. Use the same weighting system as in Step 2(c).

Some Conclusions About The Experts

Experts As To Liability—Yours

1. If the expert scores +7 or +8 as to any essential issue or element in your case, he is likely to be decisive on it to a judge and jury. You should consider him a strong positive factor affecting calculation of your case's settlement value. If you are for plaintiff, the value increases. If you are for defendant, value decreases (civil) or your plea-bargaining or acquittal prospects improve (criminal). The witness is worth any reasonable fee he demands.
2. If he scores +5 or +6 on any issue or element, he will be persuasive on it to jury and judge and should be considered a moderately positive factor affecting case value.
3. If the score is +3 or +4, he will probably have only a slight favorable influence on your case, hardly worth a fee.
4. Finally, if the score is +2, look for another expert.

Experts As To Liability—Opponent's

1. Simply reverse the effect of the expert's presence on your case settlement value. For instance, if he scores −7 or −8, you must consider him a strongly negative factor affecting case value. If you are plaintiff, the value decreases, while if you represent defendant, value increases (civil) or your plea-bargaining strength and acquittal prospects ebb (criminal).

Experts As To Damages

1. If you represent *plaintiff* and your expert scores 7 or 8, he is a strong elevating factor on case settlement value. You should preserve him at all reasonable cost.
2. *If he scores a 2 on damages and either a 1 or 2 on his profile,* consider replacing him. If he scores a 1 on damages, be sure to replace him no matter what weight his profile carries. In either event, he represents a depressing effect on settlement value.
3. If you are for the *defendant* and your expert scores 0 or 1 on damages and either a 3 or 4 on his profile, he is a strong depressing factor on settlement value and is worth whatever fee he demands (within reason).

4. If he scores a 0 to 2 on damages but only a 1 on his profile, consider replacing him, for you can probably do better. If he scores 3 or 4 on damages, do replace him no matter how high his profile score may be.

Caveat On Experts—One Further Step To Take

Every once in a while in the experience of any lawyer dealing with expert witnesses, "skim milk masquerades as cream." An expert who scores high on the Witness Evaluation Form or similar profile turns out to be the pariah of his profession or trade, a "professional witness" whose incompetence is notorious among colleagues.

> **ACTION RULE: Before finally accepting conclusions your evaluation calculations suggest, ask other lawyers about his reputation. They will tell you if it is sour. Also call one or two members of his profession or trade known to you for their opinions of his competence.**

While results of these inquiries will not be reliable on subtleties of judgment (Are the eyes of the beholders 20/20?) they will be unerring in the case of known quacks, imposters and bunco artists who are present in every profession and community.

The Remedy: If your expert is one of this class, fire him and hire another, no matter how high he scores. You can be sure he has also been found out by your opponent who has even more incentive than you to investigate him. Instead of contributing value to your case in the opponent's eyes, the "expert" will certainly deduct from it.

WHY YOU SHOULD USE THESE EVALUATIVE TECHNIQUES

This computative approach to witness evaluation does not purport to reduce to scientific certainty an area of legal practice so beset with intangibles. It cannot be done.

But it does introduce a system of witness evaluation that is more disciplined and reliable than haphazard approaches most lawyers use. Witness impact on case settlement value, if thought about at all, is usually buried under the influence of ritual theorems, such as, "The settlement value of a negligent injury case with liability is five times special damages" . . . or . . . "A defendant charged with first degree murder should always accept an offer of a plea to manslaughter."

Such bromidic "rules of thumb" are unprofessional. Worse, they shortchange clients, for they ignore the uniqueness that sets each case apart from every other, including the vast differences in value impact among witnesses.

This evaluation method recognizes and measures those differences, enabling you to more accurately predict the outcome of your case if tried. This in turn sends you into settlement negotiations knowing the best reasonable terms to demand.

> REMEMBER: The surest way to consistently win good settlements is by making consistently accurate predictions about the outcome of your cases if they were tried and fixing settlement levels accordingly. And the only way to predict trial outcome accurately is by evaluating each factor influencing verdicts. Of all such factors, witnesses influence verdicts most.

4

Investigative Techniques
For General Use

TABLE OF CONTENTS

Investigative Techniques
For General Use

"The ins and outs of a legal career are caused mainly by the ins . . . inadequate concepts, indifferent skills, insufficient courage and insignificant effort."

INTRODUCTION TO PART II:
WINNING INVESTIGATIVE TECHNIQUES

To suggest, as many exponents of trial techniques do, that a courtroom victory is primarily attributable to what occurs there is a sensible as saying that the birth of a child is primarily attributable to what happens at the hospital. Chapters 4, 5 and 6 present techniques that will help you discover facts and evidence in the conception and gestation phases of your cases. Chapter 4 covers investigative hints for a wide variety of cases. Chapter 5 demonstrates techniques for negligence, criminal, divorce and contract cases. Chapter 6 explains how to obtain winning statements from witnesses.

CHOOSING THE BEST INVESTIGATOR

One of the commonest cliches around, "If you want a job done right, do it yourself," offers good advice for lawyers on the subject of case investigations. Unless your health is poor or some other lawyer in your firm will negotiate and try the case, there are ten reasons why you should investigate it yourself—and only one instance when you should not.

TEN REASONS FOR BEING YOUR OWN INVESTIGATOR

1. You know precisely what facts and evidence to look for from knowledge of claims and defenses that must be proved.
2. You are better able to evaluate whatever the investigation uncovers by weighing it with other facts and evidence previously learned.
3. You can take the client with you on certain phases of the investigation

(e.g., to the accident or crime scene) refresh his recollection and add to your knowledge of the events.

4. You can swiftly and accurately relate facts and evidence obtained with that already secured to determine what is still needed.

5. You enjoy the advantage of immediate, personal contact with witnesses discovered, together with the opportunity to statementize them adequately before obstacles intrude (i.e. before he disappears, becomes uncooperative or is interviewed by your opponent).

6. By personally observing the crime or accident scene (as well as the place of any important thing or event) you can better understand, credit or discredit reports and statements concerning it.

7. You can more accurately take ... or direct the taking of ... measurements and photographs which have the greatest relevance and impact on your case.

8. You will have confidence in the accuracy of investigation results that is often missing when another does the investigating.

9. You will be confident of the thoroughness of the investigation, instead of wondering whether another did all he could.

10. You will carry into negotiations, discovery proceedings and the pre-trial conference a mental image of the scene and all else your investigation entailed and so speak with more conviction and accuracy.

> ACTION RULE: Unless you are physically unable to do so (you are ill, going on vacation or in a lengthy trial) always investigate for facts and evidence yourself. If another has special capability regarding a portion of the investigation which you lack, assign him that portion and you do the rest.

Many lawyers routinely hire independent investigators believing they cannot afford losing time from their offices, without realizing they truly cannot afford losing the benefits of their own investigation. Only appellate cases are won in law offices, via research and briefing. Trial court cases are won in the field, by the gathering of evidence.

Action Example: How Personal Investigation Wins

I know an eminent criminal lawyer whose reputation is so good that most investigators would give their crepe shoes to work for him. But he shuns them, preferring to do his own investigating in every case, misdemeanors to murders.

Several years ago, he defended a man accused of burglarizing a store located in a residential neighborhood early one June morning. The lawyer deposed the State's key witness, a widow who occupied a two-story dwelling adjoining and some thirty feet from the store front. She testified that she was awakened at two in the morning by the sound of breaking glass; that she immediately looked out her bedroom window and saw the defendant about to climb through the shattered store window. He glanced around him, she said, and she had a clear view of his face under the light of a nearby street lamp.

The witness spoke with calm assurance, wore no glasses, demonstrated good vision and seemed unassailable. Defense counsel was about to cut short his questioning when he suddenly remembered something he had observed while visiting the crime scene several weeks before. *There was a mature tree standing between the house and store.* He asked her about it but she denied it obstructed her view. She had no trouble seeing through it, she said, and invited him to come to her house and "see for himself."

He went and found she was right. It was November, now, the tree was bare of leaves. The view was perfect. But the crime occurred in June.

On the strength of this information, defense counsel moved and was granted a continuance of trial until the following June. Never was the leafing process observed with more interest. The tree turned out to be a maple of more than usual vigor and long before June came, the case went, "nolled" by the prosecution.

Had this lawyer not examined the scene personally, it is doubtful the tree would have come to his attention before trial. And then, it is doubtful the judge would have granted a continuance, with his jury sworn and the trial underway.

How To Select A Substitute Investigator When You Need Him

Apart from special exigencies that sometimes weigh upon every lawyer, there is one occasion when you should always choose another investigator ... *when, by reason of unique training, background or experience, he is certain to perform some phase of the investigation better than you.*

Five Investigative Jobs That Should Be Given To A Specialist:

1. *Personal surveillance.* There are competent, licensed detective agencies in every community that provide round-the-clock surveillance of adverse parties in divorce and injury cases, gathering evidence of misconduct in the first and malingering in the second.
2. *Gaining access to records which you are denied.* Many private investigators across the country are former law enforcement officers (e.g.,

Research Associates, Inc., a national concern with a nucleus of ex F.B.I. agents). They have links with police agencies that often enable them to see and report on records not accessible to you or the public generally.

3. *High quality photographing and filming of places and persons to produce evidence exhibits and for demonstration purposes.* Skilled forensic photographers and filmers operate in most urban locales, producing exhibits high in resolution and low in distortion. They can depict an injured client, a product defect or crime scene anomaly (blow-ups are especially effective) far more persuasively than you . . . no matter how good an amateur you are.

4. *Interviewing a witness with whom he has a personal relationship.* Perhaps you have tried interviewing an important police witness (e.g., the investigating officer) and been rebuffed. An independent investigator with a police background can often succeed where you failed, because of the same link that gains him access to non-public records.

5. *Witness tracing out-of-town.* There are investigators who belong to a network of offices across the country and who can trace a departed (not deceased) witness to his present location faster and more economically than you.

Checklist For Choosing The Best Independent Investigator

—*Phone several investigators* from the list of those advertising in the yellow pages of your telephone directory under the headings "Investigator" and "Detective Agencies" ("Photographer" if that is what you need).

—*Obtain the following information from each:* his experience, training, vocational background (as they relate to the specific job you want done); whether he is licensed by the State and municipality; whether he is bonded against mis- or malfeasance and by whom.

—*Describe in detail the job you want him to do* (without naming names) and obtain a fee quote, preferably a flat fee for the job.

—*Determine whether any one investigator you call has special qualifications* for your job not shared by the others (e.g., he retired from the police department involved in your case).

—*Ask him for names of other lawyers for whom he has worked.*

—*Ask for a guarantee* that he will apply himself to your job and complete it within the time it must be done, stating a deadline.

—*After obtaining the foregoing information* from each investigator, call the attorneys each named as prior employers. Explain that you contemplate hiring the investigator, ask what services he performed for the other and how he performed them. Finally, ask each attorney whether he would hire the investigator again if a similar need arose.

—*After you perform each of the previous steps,* compare the investigators on the basis of information gathered *and choose the one who combines the greatest number of the following:* He is licensed and bonded; is recommended by another lawyer for the job you need done; has special qualifications for the job; has general qualifications for the job; pledges to do the job immediately and quotes the lowest flat fee (or lowest hourly fee if none quotes a flat basis).

At the opposite pole from the lawyer who never conducts his own investigation, because he believes he cannot afford the time, stands the lawyer who never hires an independent investigator because he believes he cannot afford the fee. Or because he believes advancing the fee is unethical. The first belief is a false concept, the second is false economy, and the third is simply false.

If you limit his use to special situations when he is most effective and select him by means of techniques discussed, the outside investigator usually returns much more value than the fee he receives. The difference between hiring and not hiring him is often the difference between winning and not winning, for in many of the cases you handle, it takes but little additional evidence to satisfy preponderance and reasonable doubt tests.

THE ETHICS OF ADVANCING EXPENSES

May a lawyer pay an investigator's fee out of his own pocket when the client is unable to pay it himself? This is a question that has troubled and divided lawyers and Bar Associations for years. On the one hand is the argument that by doing so the lawyer is financing the litigation, an offense even in Roman times. Champerty was always a "cussword" in legal lexicons.

On the other hand is the equally strong argument that in many instances unless the lawyer pays (or at least guarantees payment) the investigation will not be made, the evidence not obtained and the case not won.

The question was recently answered by the American Bar Association in its Code of Professional Responsibility: The lawyer may pay an investigator's fee as an advancement, with ultimate liability for the fee resting with the client, who shall reimburse the lawyer subsequently.

Disciplinary Rule #5-103(B): "While representing a client in connection with a contemplated or pending litigation, a lawyer shall not advance or guarantee financial assistance to his client, *except that a lawyer may advance or guarantee the expenses of litigation, including court costs, expenses of investigation, expenses of medical examination, and costs of obtaining and presenting evidence, provided the client remains ultimately liable for such expenses.*"

HOW TO IDENTIFY AND LOCATE THE MISSING WITNESS

"Locating a missing witness is essential," a cynical lawyer once observed, "in order to know how badly you are going to lose."

As with all cynics, this man knows the price of everything and the value of nothing. The value of locating a missing witness lies not in his telling you anything about defeat, but in his telling you so much about victory. For if he turns out to be adverse to your case position, you can simply draw the veil about him once again and let him slide back into obscurity. But if he helps your position, you will throw the veil aside permanently, publicize his presence to your opponent, and adjust the case settlement value commensurate with his contribution (upward if you are for plaintiff, downward if for defendant).

Dealing With The Two Types of Missing Witnesses

There are two classes of missing witnesses to consider. First is the witness whose identity is known but not his whereabouts. He gave his name and address to somebody connected with the case (e.g., client, investigating officer, another witness) but when you seek him at his house, you find him moved.

The other type is one who is known or suspected to exist but is nameless. He is the driver of the car who tells those at the accident scene he saw what happened, then leaves before his identity is established. Or he is the bystander at the event scene who is observed but communicates to no one.

There are special techniques for finding both types. All involve effort, but the potential reward is usually more than ample compensation!

Checklist For Locating A Missing Witness Whose Identity Is Known

1. *Check the telephone directory* and call his listed number. If he moved within the same exchange area, he may have the same number.
2. *If the listed number* is not working, call the "information" operator for his new number, then call it for his new address.
3. *If unsuccessful, consult a street directory* ("criss-cross") of recent issue. It may have an alphabetical index of all occupants listed, tagged to the page where each can be found. Telephone companies and independent publishers print such directories for use by business establishments and professionals. If you cannot find one, call or visit your local library, which probably has it.

4. *If unsuccessful, visit his old neighborhood* and interview neighbors on either side and across the street. If they do not know his new address, ask for personal information that will aid your search (e.g., his employer, children and ages, wife and her employer, names and addresses of local relatives, church attended, organization memberships).

5. *Follow up leads* given you by neighbors. Contact his employer, relatives, friends, closest schools (if school-age children) church pastor and membership chairmen of his organizations.

6. *If still unsuccessful, mail a certified letter* to the witness' old address, "return receipt requested, showing address where delivered". Should the letter be returned undelivered, visit the post office (a phone call will gain nothing) and ask for his forwarding address. Explain your need of him and you will occasionally receive a sympathetic, and informative, response. If this fails, seek out the letter carrier who served him for the new address. He is often less a stickler for postal rules.

7. *If further investigating is necessary,* do the following: Contact the utility companies serving his old residence. They will have his new address if he moved within their franchise area. Even if the move is outside it, they may have a forwarding address for the final bill, and return of deposit.

8. *Contact real estate brokers* nearby his old address, if it is a private residence. One may have sold the house and knows the new address. If he does not know it, ask him for the name and address of the escrow company that closed the sale transaction and contact it for the address to which closing papers were mailed.

9. *Contact the local office of the State Board of Elections* (or under whatever other name it may be known). A new registration by the witness is recorded here.

10. *Contact local savings and loan companies.* Chances are good he continued his savings account, with instructions to mail interest earnings to him.

11. *Contact the motor vehicle department* of your State, driver's license division. Many States pick up and return to the issuing State the old license of a new resident applicant. The appropriate agency of the latter will have a record of the transmitting office.

12. *If all else fails, contact local department stores* where the witness and wife are likely to have shopped (on credit). The accounts or credit departments may have a forwarding address.

How Knowledge Of Habits Can Help

Sometimes you will learn the city but not the street address to which the witness moved, and be unable to trace him using these techniques. In this event, knowing his habits may be the key to finding him.

Not long ago, I watched a televized interview of the head of a nationwide missing persons bureau. He claimed 100% success in locating people who disappeared and still lived.

"Nobody can hide himself from discovery very long," he said, "even when he tries. *His habits betray him.*"

It is a truth for all investigators to remember. Learn what your witness' habits are from relatives, friends and neighbors (e.g., religious, recreational, political, organizational, avocational habits) then inquire of appropriate institutions in the new city for him.

FINDING THE UNKNOWN WITNESS

Locating a witness whose identity is not known poses more of a problem. He is like the proverbial needle ... but with this important difference: you know the precise place in the haystack where he once was. If he was a bystander at the place where your event occurred (accident or crime scene) he may still be somewhere nearby. Or, if he was in a passing car, there is a good chance he followed a repeated route ... and still does.

Here is a checklist of steps you should take before deeming him permanently lost.

Checklist For Finding A Witness Who Is Not Known

1. If the witness was a bystander or you do not know how he got there, always canvass the neighborhood of the scene. If it is a residential neighborhood, question all available occupants of every house on both sides of the street and in both directions from the event site. If a business neighborhood, question all available employees (be sure to get the employer's consent) at each nearby establishment. A good rule of thumb to use for placing geographical limits is to check out every structure within possible sight or hearing of the event.
   —*Time your canvass* to coincide with the hour when the event occurred (also the same day of the week, if possible) to profit from the chance that the witness is usually in the neighborhood then.
   —*Tell each person* you question the importance of your search; that a witness may make the difference and lead to a just case result. Then briefly describe the event and ask him if he knows anything about it.

(Do not ask if he "witnessed" it. He will answer "no" and still have witnessed important post-event facts, such as skid marks, vehicle locations, crime scene physical conditions or admissions by the adverse party.)

—*Always ask* each person you question if anyone discussed the event with him in a way that suggested the other person witnessed it, or personally knew some fact connected with it. If someone did, get his name and address, suspend your canvass and seek to question him immediately.

—*Ask each person* you question if another person at his home or business place, but not now present, was in the building or neighborhood when the event occurred. If there was, get his name and telephone number and call him later.

2. If an account of the event appeared in a local newspaper, interview the reporter who wrote the story. An experienced investigator himself, he is often more thorough than policemen in beating the bushes for witnesses. If he found one, his notes will yield the witness' identity.

3. Question people who are known to have been at the scene but whom you have not interviewed (e.g., policemen who assisted the investigating officer, ambulance or tow truck drivers, building or street repairmen, utility repairmen, newspapermen, news or free-lance photographers).

4. Question people who are regularly at or near the scene at the day and hour of the event (e.g., mail man, milk man, rubbish collector, home delivery man, newspaper boy). You can find out who they are from building occupants you question.

5. If the case warrants the expense, place a small ad in the local newspaper several days in succession. Have it spotted on a news page and not with classified ads. (How often do you read the "personal" column?) For a few extra dollars you can surround the ad with a heavy, black border and make it much more distinguishable.

6. If the expense is warranted, buy spot announcements on a local radio station, several days running. Specify 7-9 A.M. and 4-6 P.M. time slots when the audience is largest.

7. If the witness was in a car and its license plate number is known, trace the owner through the police department, local office of the American Automobile Association, or State motor vehicle department. It helps if you belong to AAA, and are friendly with the police or motor vehicles office, but even if you are not, an explanation of your search is usually enough to win fast cooperation.

8. If the event occurred shortly before or after a normal shift change (commonly 7 a.m., 3 p.m. and 11 p.m.) and the witness was in a car, contact all industries in the area. Explain the importance of your search

and ask for an announcement over the public address system, a notice on plant bulletin boards or an ad in the plant newspaper (preferably all three).

Of all these search techniques, the neighborhood canvass is usually the most productive. Every veteran lawyer with whom I have discussed fact investigations emphasized its importance, for each had the experience of discovering witnesses by its means who never would have surfaced otherwise. On the negative side, canvassing is time-consuming, plodding, and often discouraging work. You may prefer sending an independent investigator to do it . . . or a young attorney in your office. If you do, be sure to instruct him to be thorough and skip no building within the zone you define.

HOW TO SEARCH OUT FACTS USING SUBTERFUGE

"There are some things about you even your best friends won't tell you."

Not too many years ago, a major merchandiser of mouthwash scored impressive sales on the strength of this slogan. And it is true, in the case of halitosis. But it is also true that there are other things about you that your best friends will tell others . . . and so will your neighbors.

Neighbors of the adverse party are often a fertile source of helpful information about him, discrediting both his claims and himself. When approached just right, some will disclose it, more often than is commonly realized. And that disclosure may be enough to badly blemish an otherwise flawless case, driving settlement value down or elevating it (depending on whether you represent defendant or plaintiff).

> **ACTION RULE:** Whenever you suspect the adverse party is lying about or grossly exaggerating a liability or damage contention, arrange for an interview of his residence neighbors to achieve these two objectives: 1) Identify the lie or exaggeration, thus enabling you to secure evidence of facts refuting it (e.g., films revealing a false disability claim). 2) Secure a witness who can refute the claim on the basis of what he has seen or was told by the adverse party.

There are a multitude of facts in many types of cases that neighbors will sometimes know and tell. Here are a few that come most readily to mind from my own experience.

Examples Of Discoverable Truths

—How the accident occurred, as told by the adverse party to his neighbor (negligence cases). Here the party may be plaintiff or defendant.

—Details of the alleged crime, as told by the complaining witness to his neighbor (criminal cases).

—The nature and extent of personal injury and disability, as described by the plaintiff to his neighbor and/or as observed by the latter (negligence, assault and product liability cases).

—The nature and extent of damage to real and personal property, as described by the plaintiff to his neighbor and/or as observed by the latter (negligence, trespass and nuisance cases).

—The nature and extent of special damages incurred (e.g., medical expenses, earnings or profits loss, loss of rent, loss of use, cost of substitute performance) as told to the neighbor by the plaintiff.

—The condition of real and personal property prior to events causing damage and the cost of acquisition, as described by the plaintiff to his neighbor and as observed by the latter (negligence, trespass and nuisance cases).

—Knowledge of a superior title holder, as admitted by an adverse possessor of land to his neighbor (quiet title, ejectment or declaratory judgment actions).

—Facts concerning child abuse or neglect, financial needs or income, claimed aggression or spousal misconduct, as described by either party to a neighbor (divorce or alimony/separation cases).

—Details of non-identification or police induced identification, as told by a prosecution witness to his neighbor (criminal cases).

Ideas In Action: When The Neighbors Told All

I recall two cases in which settlement values nosedived because of statements given defense investigators by neighbors of the plaintiffs. One was an auto negligence case with unquestioned liability resting on defendant. The impact was severe and plaintiff sustained ligamentous strain to his back which defense doctors conceded were legitimate. But plaintiff also claimed permanent partial disability to his back which caused him agonizing pain (he said) on forward bending. This the defense doctors found no objective basis for.

Still, the claim had medical support and the defense knew it faced an uphill struggle refuting it. Then an investigator was sent to interview neighbors, and it was suddenly all downhill. It seems the neighbor's bedroom faced plaintiff's rose garden, to which the latter was passionately devoted. The neighbor thought it odd that many early mornings when he dressed for work, he saw plaintiff exit his back door burdened with garden tools, look furtively around as though bent on a crime, then busy himself in his roses . . . *bending low to the ground all the while.*

The case was settled for the price of a simple back sprain.

The second case was based on negligent plumbing installation consisting of an inadequately insulated water pipe running through an outside wall. One cold winter night while claimant and family were away, the pipe burst and several hundred gallons inundated his recreation room.

Claimant submitted a demand of $2,000 for replacing 8 pieces of furniture he said were brand new, together with receipts from a furniture store purporting to verify the claim. All looked in order . . . until a neighbor two doors away was questioned. Here is how the questioning went:

"I understand Mr. Payne's brand new recreation room furniture was ruined in his flood a while back," the investigator commented.

"Huh," snorted the neighbor. "I saw that stuff and it was junk. He told me himself his mother gave it to him rather than take it to Goodwill."

Further investigation revealed that the furniture dealer was an accomodating friend who had given claimant several receipt forms without questioning their intended use. When confronted with these facts, claimant hurriedly accepted $200 in full settlement.

Similar instances are legion and point up the devastating effect this procedure can have on seemingly unassailable cases.

CHECKLIST FOR OBTAINING USEFUL FACTS
FROM NEIGHBORS

1. *Hire an independent investigator* to do the interviewing, using selection procedures presented earlier in this Chapter. Here is where the subterfuge enters. You should not be identified with the interview. If the neighbor learns that his information is sought for lawsuit purposes, he is reluctant

to talk at all or reveal the truth. He fears the very thing that always happens when helpful facts are disclosed . . . the adverse party learns who disclosed it. Further, he fears becoming embroiled in litigation and will keep the truth you need concealed rather than risk involvement.

For these reasons, you dare not question neighbors yourself nor send an office associate to do it. Even if you or he are willing to lie about your identity and purpose, it is bad policy (bad ethics, too). They are sure to remember your masquerade and embarass you with it in the courtroom ("He told me he was making a credit study.").

2. *If you cannot find an investigator with experience* interviewing under subterfuge, contact the local office of the Retail Credit Company or a local company doing like work. Retail Credit is a national concern which investigates the insurability, employability or credit status of people, largely by means of interviewing their neighbors. Although its work is almost entirely for business concerns, staff investigators sometimes free lance.

3. *Meet the investigator you hire before he begins* interviewing and insist that he not disclose your identity nor the real purpose of the interview. If he is experienced, he will know enough not to anyway. But it is prudent to make sure. He knows ways of explaining his mission and asking questions that avoid implicating you and your case (e.g., He may say simply that he is investigating the man next door's claim arising from injuries he suffered, leaving it to the neighbor to conclude what type of claim it is. The latter will likely think it is an industrial, unemployment or accident and health claim, or one under some insurance of his own).

4. *Supply the investigator with a factual background* of your case, together with your contentions and the adverse party's contentions concerning it. Then specify the areas of possible lies or exaggeration of the latter, so the investigator knows what subjects to zero in on during the interviews.

5. *Ask him to submit a written report* to you following his interviews containing the following: name, address, age, employment and brief physical description of each neighbor interviewed; location of the neighbor's house in relation to that of the adverse party; a summary of information obtained from each interviewee; a detailed statement in the interviewee's own words bearing on any subject you specified in the previous step.

6. *Tell him that whenever he obtains information that seems to confirm a lie or exaggeration* you suspected, he should try to obtain a written statement signed by the interviewee. (He can explain to the interviewee that he needs it for his file.) The statement serves two purposes in case you cannot settle the case and must call the neighbor as a witness at trial:

It refreshes his recollection, and it guards against his changing his story and denying he ever said it. There is a third purpose. You can use it for effective cross-examination should he appear for the adverse party on another subject.

7. *Instruct the investigator* that if he elicits helpful information from a neighbor, he should ask whether the other intends moving in the near future (within the next two years). If the answer is "yes", he should then learn the new address (at least the city) if it is known *and* names and addresses of close relatives here.

8. *Finally, tell him not to antagonize any interviewee;* that if the latter refuses to talk about the adverse party, the investigator should leave without arguing.

DISCOVERING FACTS
WITHOUT HAVING TO USE DISCOVERY

Many facts vital to case success or failure are never unearthed in time to influence settlement negotiations, because counsel does not know where to dig for them. Or knowing where, does not know how.

Few lawyers seem aware, for example, that each office of the U.S. Weather Bureau publishes a monthly chart of local weather phenomena, itemized on a daily basis, which is available on request for a nominal fee. Yet many cases turn on weather conditions on the day of crucial events. Whether the wind was as strong as plaintiff claims or the rain as heavy as defendant contends are often central questions on which victory for one or the other pivots.

Action Example: When Untimely Proof Is No Proof At All

I remember a fall-down case that came to trial in my court. Plaintiff claimed that as she entered the front door of Zayre's Department store on a shopping errand, she slipped and fell in a puddle of water that had been tracked in from a rain shower. Defendant store allowed the water to accumulate, she asserted, thereby failing to exercise due care for business invitees.

Witnesses for both sides testified contrarily on the subject of water inside the store, but defense counsel offered no evidence on the question whether there was water outside it . . . until after a verdict was rendered for plaintiff for $20,000. Then he filed a motion for a new trial based on newly discovered evidence. It seems that after the trial, he secured a Weather Bureau chart for the day in question showing *absolutely no rainfall within a 20 mile radius of the store.*

I denied the motion for the reason that this evidence could have been discovered in time for the trial, had counsel been properly diligent. (The judgment was affirmed on appeal.)

There is no doubt in my mind that had the weather data been secured before trial, as it should, the case could have been settled substantially below the verdict.

LEARNING FIRST IF YOU CAN COLLECT A JUDGMENT

Many lawyers who are zealous pursuers of liability and damage facts pay no attention to a defendant's financial condition, with these common results; 1) They win handsome judgments that are never collected, or 2) They accept defense counsel's representations of poverty and settle too cheaply.

In a non-insurance case (no insurance coverage that will pay the judgment) pursuing a defendant to judgment without ascertaining his finances is akin to pursuing a woman with marriage in mind, without ascertaining if she is single. It's actually worse, for in the case of a married woman, she might free herself by divorce, but an indigent defendant can usually be counted on to free himself from the judgment by bankruptcy.

There was an alienation of affections action that made the front page in many newspapers. "Abandoned wife wins $30,000," one caption read. What readers never knew was that the case could have been settled for $1,000 before trial. The money was coming from a relative, defense counsel said, warning that his client was penniless.

"I've heard that line before," responded plaintiff's lawyer at the pre-trial conference. Had he checked defendant out? No, but "I've reason to think he can pay much more," he said. So, although the wife was inclined to take the offer and spare herself the embarassment of testifying, her lawyer would have none of it. He handled the trial well and won the $30,000 judgment. After the trial he exulted, "I've fixed that s.o.b."

Three years later he has yet to collect dime one.

ACTION RULE: Unless insurance coverage is available to pay whatever judgment you can reasonably expect to win, always investigate a defendant's financial condition before entering settlement negotiations or determining to proceed with suit or trial. Then, treat that condition as an important factor influencing the settlement value of your case.

Here is a compilation of fact sources arranged according to whether they relate to liability issues, damage or remedy issues or the defendant's financial status.

CHECKLIST OF FACT SOURCES—LIABILITY ISSUES

—*Police motor vehicle accident reports.* Police departments throughout the country require an official accident report prepared by the investigating officer(s) whenever the latter is called to the scene to investigate. The reports are on file with the department and are public records. If the accident occurred in an unincorporated section, the investigating agency will likely be either the county sheriff or state police.

—*Other police reports.* The policy of most police departments throughout the country is to require an official, filed report of every investigation any officer makes while in the scope of his employment. Consequently, if he responds to a marital dispute, a flare-up between neighbors over property lines, an assault and battery, an industrial accident, etc., there will probably be a report on file in his department that you should inspect.

—*County recorder or land title office.* Has photostat or microfilm copies of deeds, mortgages, land contracts (if required to be filed) and leases. Also is custodian of plats for sub-divisions. Usually maintains street maps of all land within the county showing names of current and previous owners, together with the volume and page of the deed record where the conveyance may be found.

—*Clerk of courts.* The Clerk of each court maintains a record of every case filed, its progress and disposition. They are cross-indexed alphabetically under the names of both plaintiff and defendant for ready access. Pleadings are preserved, as is the judgment order. Consult for, among other things, prior divorces, litigation and arrest and conviction history of the adverse party. In a motor vehicle case where an arrest was made, consult traffic court records for the disposition of the case.

—*Printed advertising literature, television, radio and newspaper ads.* Such materials often contain representations of quality, performance and safety of the products they tout, constituting express warranties which, upon breach, impose liability upon their makers.

—*Newspaper stories, newsreel films and video tapes of persons and scenes; broadcast and televized interviews with principals and witnesses.* Names of unknown witnesses and impeaching statements by the adverse party can sometimes be found. Accident and crime scenes may be depicted here soon after the events. Consult the "morgue" (clipping library) of your local newspapers, where stories are indexed and preserved according to subject matter. Check with the program directors of your television stations to see if your event was covered and aired. They are required by the F.C.C. to keep descriptive records of everything broadcast and may still have the video tape.

—*Coroner's inquest records and/or autopsy report.* Whenever you have a civil or criminal case in which death figures, consult the coroner's office to learn whether he took evidence or conducted an autopsy of the victim to determine the cause of death. The records and reports are commonly public records.

—*Death certificates.* Most states require a decedent's treating physician to certify in writing the cause of death, then file same with a state or county agency where it becomes a public record. (The state or county Board of Health or Department of Vital Statistics is a common agency name.) If the certified cause confirms your claim, it is a positive influence on settlement value. If it disagrees with your claim, it is a negative influence.

—*Weather reports.* Detailed daily records of temperature, precipitation and wind conditions are required to be kept by each office of the U.S. Weather Bureau. Monthly compilations can be ordered by mail for a small fee.

—*Fire department, State Fire Marshal or Arson Bureau reports.* Whenever your case involves fire damage and fire department action, obtain a copy of the official department report. It normally describes the fire, its effect, and its cause, and contains an estimate of the dollar loss. If arson is suspected, the State or local agency having authority will investigate and report separately. You can obtain a copy directly from the agency.

—*Hospital records.* Hospitals will not allow access or supply copies of their treatment records without a signed authorization from the patient or court order. If you represent plaintiff, you should have your client sign enough authorizations for each hospital and clinic that examined and/or treated him. (See Chapter 1 for a sample form.)

If you represent defendant, you can often learn what the record on plaintiff contains through the agency of another doctor. Do you have a friend who is a doctor, having privileges at the hospital? Do you regularly use the same doctor for defense examinations? Then ask him to pull plaintiff's file and report essentials. *The history of the accident as given by plaintiff to the receiving doctor or nurse is what you are interested in.* It is a time and circumstance when nearly everybody is truthful. Thoughts are on physical rather than financial recovery. His account of events may exonerate defendant altogether, or so diverge from later statements as to discredit him.

—*Interstate Commerce Commission records.* If the accident you are investigating involved a truck or bus which regularly crosses State lines, request a copy of the driver's report from the office of the I.C.C. nearest the scene. Under recently adopted regulations, all accidents resulting in personal injury or substantial property damage must be reported in detail.

—*State motor vehicle accident reports.* Current laws of most States require each driver involved in an accident causing personal injury or property damage in excess of a specified amount (commonly $100 or $500) to file a detailed report with the State motor vehicle department, on its forms. You can obtain a copy on written request of the agency and payment of a nominal fee ($1 or $2). Since there is normally a time deadline for filing it, the parties often complete the forms themselves, creating leads to impeachment.

—*Agreement with opposing counsel.* The easiest and fastest way to obtain facts and copies of documents which you lack and your opponent has is to ask him for them. You should always do so. The worst is that he refuses, which leaves you where you were. *But he will ordinarily not refuse,* if relations are reasonably good and trial is not imminent, for he wants something from you . . . a settlement.

   You can ordinarily obtain the following classes of facts by merely asking; hospital, medical and dental reports and bills; inspection of real and personal property; repair estimates and bills concerning real and personal property; copies of correspondence, contracts, invoices, accounts and other records figuring in your case; copies of photographs of persons, places and things.

   In criminal cases you can often get your client's past criminal history; handwriting samples the State's expert relies upon; inspection of contraband the prosecutor holds; access to drugs for your own chemical tests; access to the weapon for your own ballistics, trigger pull or metallurgical tests.

CHECKLIST OF FACT SOURCES—
DAMAGE OR REMEDY ISSUES

—*Police accident and fire reports.* They generally contain estimates of damage according to the opinion of the officer reporting.

—*School reports and records.* If the claimant is school age, look at his attendance, health and scholastic records at schools attended before and after the accident. Claims about the effects of his injury may be refuted by the older records, showing poor attendance, health and scholarship before the accident, too.

—*Hospital and clinic records.* Obtain through the doctor contact, again. Examine "Onset of Symptoms," "Patient's History," "Report of Examination," and "Provisional and Final Diagnosis" sections for facts that strengthen your claim or defense. If you are for plaintiff, look at "Nurses Notes" which records the hourly progress (or regress) of the client, his complaints of pain and medication administered for it.

> REMEMBER: Whether you represent plaintiff or defendant, do not be satisfied with only the records of current treatment. Try to get prior hospital and clinic records on the plaintiff as well, that may prove that his physical condition is chronic rather than recently caused.

—*State motor vehicle and Interstate Commerce Commission accident reports.* They contain estimates of property damage and personal injury by the client and adverse party and often sharply disagree with present contentions.

—*Estimates by repairers not used by claimant.* Although claimants in real or personal property damage cases normally obtain several repair estimates, they always base their claims on the highest among them. If you represent defendant in such cases, you can often find the lowest estimator and save yourself the expense of hiring one. Inquire by phone using the same procedure plaintiff used . . . refer to the telephone book yellow pages for the listing of repairmen in the specialty involved (auto mechanic, body shop, carpenter, plumber, roofer, etc.) and choose 3 or 4 nearby plaintiff's premises. Call each one and when you locate a lower estimate, obtain a copy.

—*Personnel and payroll records.* If you represent defendant in a case wherein plaintiff claims loss of wages, write the payroll office of his employer for an itemization of missed days, *before and after* the accident, his hourly rate and work duties. Refer in your letter to the necessity of deposing the records if information is refused. The information will often be forthcoming, it will be accurate and it may contradict one or more of plaintiff's claims.

It is sometimes possible to gain access to plaintiff's medical chart in his employer's personnel office on the strength of the same deposition threat. His medical background, injury history, and industrial claims, if any, are recorded here and can be a fruitful source of impeachment.

—*Agreement with opposing counsel.* As with liability issue facts, many facts and documents relating to damage issues can be secured from your opponent by simply asking for them. Repair bills and estimates, medical and hospital bills and reports are some of the documents that can be easily obtained this way.

CHECKLIST OF FACT SOURCES— DEFENDANT'S FINANCIAL STATUS

—*County deeds, mortgages, lease, lien records.* Always check the deed indexes in the county where plaintiff resides for proof of real estate ownership. If you find it, then examine mortgage book indexes and lien records to find all encumbrances that reduce his equity.

—*Court judgment records.* Examine the judgment lien indexes at the proper custodian office within his residence county. They will usually be found in the same office where deed, mortgage, and mechanic's lien records are stored. Also, you can probably find them at the clerk of the general jurisdiction trial court's office within the county. Learn the number and amount of unsatisfied money judgments against defendant.

—*Automobile title registration office records.* Check indexes of the county car title office to learn what vehicles he owns and mortgages against them, if any.

—*Payroll records.* Defendant's monthly gross and net wages can be learned here; also whether deductions are taken for credit union purposes, which may mean either a loan debt or a savings credit.

—*Bank records.* A call to the bookkeeping offices of local commercial banks can often disclose whether he has checking accounts and the average monthly balance carried (in rough figures). Do not identify yourself as an attorney and the clerk will assume you call from the credit office of a retail store or that you hold a check of its depositor. She will then tell you that his balance averages two, three, or four figures (tens, hundreds, or thousands of dollars).

—*Information from opposing counsel.* Whenever you represent plaintiff for money damages, whether there is liability insurance coverage afforded the defendant or not, you should always ask defense counsel what assets would be available to pay a judgment . . . assuming you obtained one. Ask him before you begin settlement negotiations so there is time to verify what he tells you and factor it into your case evaluation.

—*Insurance available.* Counsel may not tell you policy limits because he does not know them, or he knows them, but they are high and he does not wish to encourage you by revealing them. If counsel does not know limits, he will tell you so. If he does not deny knowing them and will not reveal them, it is a reliable indication that policy limits are ample for your case. And you should treat this silence about limits as a positive factor influencing your determination of case settlement value.

Note: Also be sure to ask defense counsel (who was probably hired by the insurance company) whether the company claims a policy defense. If it does, learn the facts and legal principles supporting the claim so you can judge whether the defense, too, should be a factor (negative) influencing settlement value.

Note: More plaintiffs' counsel are learning policy limits before filing suit than ever before, because of liberalized discovery rules in state and federal courts. In the federal jurisdiction and in those many states with comparable procedural rules, you can learn all provisions of the policy by using regular discovery tools. (See Chapter 13 for rules and techniques). Knowing you can discover the limits after suit, insurance companies are often willing to tell you them beforehand to expedite settlement and save them the expense of hiring counsel.

—*No insurance available.* As insurance counsel will normally tell you policy limits when they are low, so non-insurance counsel will normally tell you defendant's assets when they are little. Do not accept what he says at face value. Demand documentation where appropriate (e.g., copy of the deed showing title in another; copy of the mortgage against his property; wage stubs showing gross earnings and deductions; demands from creditors showing bills owed). Investigate his facts (e.g., look for a later deed or cancelled mortgage). Whatever information defense counsel gives you may be more than you can get yourself . . . and will speed your investigation . . . so be sure to ask him for it.

—*Personal observation.* Besides investigating the state of title and encumbrances in defendant's house, look it over yourself or ask your client to do it. Call any real estate broker nearby the house, identify and describe it, and you can learn about what it will sell for. Deduct total encumbrances, allow for divided ownership, and you have the value of defendant's equity. Do the same for any business place defendant owns, following it with a search of county records for conditional sales or mortgage agreements encumbering his inventory and fixtures.

Winning Techniques For Investigating Particular Civil Or Criminal Cases

TABLE OF CONTENTS

5

Winning Techniques
For Investigating Particular
Civil Or Criminal Cases

"Investigating an accident scene for evidence is like fishing Lake Erie. You're never sure you'll get any and, if you do, whether it will be worth having." Judge Thomas D. Lambros.

Motor vehicle accident cases and criminal defenses are still two of the most common areas of your work, despite recent events in the areas of no-fault insurance and indigent rights. And one of the most common reasons these cases are lost or settled unfavorably is "that last missing clue we couldn't find." This chapter covers investigative techniques for these types of cases that will help you find *all* of the evidence you need.

In today's legal world when judges are prone to observe, "There's less here than meets the ear," facts count for more than eloquence and investigative skill is worth more than rhetorical skill. Match the callowest law school grad having good investigative techniques against a Cicero of the Bar who limits his work to the courtroom, and the former will win more often than lose. Here is an actual case that proves this point and shows how you can apply the techniques discussed here.

Action Example—How Industry Can Defeat Experience

Several years ago, a novice and a veteran lawyer were matched against each other in an auto negligence case, with the novice representing plaintiff. It was a side-swipe case with each driver claiming the other crossed the center line of the road and caused the collision.

Although plaintiff's injuries were extensive, the case seemed headed for a nominal settlement because of a lack of proof. The only witnesses were occupants of the cars who, naturally, favored their respective drivers. The investigating police officer could not fix the point of impact because debris was scattered over a wide area at the center of the road, as much on one side of center line as on the other.

On the eve of a pre-trial conference a modest settlement offer was made, accompanied by the veteran lawyer's kindly admonition to "grab it before it's withdrawn." Fully expecting that grab it he would, yet unhappy at settling so cheaply, plaintiff's counsel decided to complete his investigation by examining defendant's car at a junkyard where it had been since the accident.

Counsel looked the car over and saw just what he had expected, extensive left side damage from the side-swipe. But there was one other thing that had escaped the police officer's notice. The left front tire was flat. Did it collapse in the collision or after the car was towed in? The yard operator could not say. If it collapsed in the collision, could the wheel rim have marked the pavement?

Counsel returned to the accident scene for answers to his own questions, not really expecting anything helpful because he had been to the scene months before without finding anything. But in the words of the song, it *was* better the second time around. Close scrutiny of the pavement surface discovered a six-inch long groove in the asphalt, about 18 inches from the center line *and in plaintiff's lane.* Counsel photographed his find with a poloroid camera and made a gift of the print to his opponent the next day at the conference.

With a big assist from the judge (who remarked that the picture was conclusive in his eyes) the case was settled at ten times the original offer. Had counsel decided not to complete his investigation, he would have settled for the lower offer. No word of criticism would have been spoken, no disciplinary proceeding or malpractice suit would have been commenced against him. *Yet his client would have been deprived of an adequate recovery as surely as if some lawyer blunder had cost him the difference.*

ACTION RULE: **Always perform every step of your case investigation before settling it. Take all the time you need and do not be intimated by a stated deadline for acceptance of an offer. Unless trial is imminent, the offer will remain open, ultimatum notwithstanding. Avoid making a firm offer of settlement until your investigation is completed. It is difficult to increase an offer once made (if you are for plaintiff) or reduce it (if you are for** defendant) to reflect new and favorable evidence without antagonizing your opponent and losing the settlement option.

Section A.   INVESTIGATING ACCIDENT CASES

HOW TO INVESTIGATE THE ACCIDENT SCENE

One need not be a Sherlock Holmes to derive valuable information from an accident scene, for there are always many more clues to be found there than were ever available to Mr. Holmes. All that is required is that you know what to look for and how to go about finding and preserving it. Does your case involve a two-car collision? The pavement may reveal their positions at impact and the paths they followed after. Is it a right-of-way case? The scene may reveal view obstructions or impairment. Is a traffic light involved? Examination of the light may show an improper sequence, an overlapping green or a malfunctioning caution. Is excessive speed claimed? Skid marks may enable you to prove or refute the claim. Or you may find a nearby speed sign the adverse party disregarded.

> ACTION RULE: Always visit the accident scene at least once before assigning a settlement value to your case. It serves two purposes; 1) To search for helpful evidence, and 2) To familiarize yourself with the scene so as to understand and remember the evidence better. Take your client with you to help with measurements and provide background information as an aid to your search (i.e., his recollection of the point of impact, routes of the vehicles before and after, etc.) Even if you represent an insured defendant and a company adjuster previously investigated the scene, do it again yourself. Adjusters have heavy work loads and are rarely thorough, either because of haste, disinclination, or ignorance of what facts are important.

Eight "Must Items" To Take Along

The following items of equipment should be taken along when you visit the scene. Each fills a need that arises in nearly every case. Some lawyers find it convenient to store them in their cars between trips to insure availability.

1. *Camera* (preferably Poloroid) with plenty of color film and flash bulbs. You will be taking pictures at many angles and distances, and Poloroid enables you to see prints at the scene and take new shots if the others are unsatisfactory, immediately. It is unnecessary to purchase an expensive

model (though the cost of whatever you buy is a business deduction). If the need arises for a more professional picture (as a court exhibit, perhaps) you should call in a professional photographer. Then, it is not so much the excellence of the camera that counts, but the excellence of the man holding it.

2. *Tape measure.* For use in measuring skid marks, width of lanes and roadways, and distances between permanent reference points to places or objects that are relevant to your case. Get a fabric tape at least 25 feet long. The shorter, metal kind is a nuisance to use and threatens to put an eye out each time you retract it.

3. *Chart paper.* For use in preparing a diagram of the scene, together with a *pencil, eraser* and *ruler* for drawing straight lines.

4. *Folding measure.* Use it to measure short distances and depths (e.g., the depth of a chuckhole or other pavement defect). For photographic purposes as a visible measure of some important dimension.

5. *Legal pad or other note paper having a stiff backing.* A notebook or bound paper having a rigid back is a must for secure and convenient note-taking. Too many lawyers make their notes on scrap paper or scribbled on file jackets and are dismayed several months later to find the scraps missing or the notes illegible.

6. *Pair of calf-height boots.* Not all scene investigations can be conducted in warm and dry weather. In fact, it has been my experience that the further I had to go from pavement, into berm, ditches or adjacent fields, the worse conditions were—mud like quicksand or bottomless snow drifts.

7. *Two road flares.* Placed 100 yards in both directions from where you are working on a roadway, they are as good as a barricade for shielding you from injury.

8. *Large flashlight.* Especially during winter, night sometimes descends before your investigation is complete and a flashlight is essential to make the last measurements or note entries. It is also useful for examining dark corners, shadowed places and inside automobiles and other objects.

Here is a list of important steps to take when investigating at the scene of an accident. A neighborhood canvass for witnesses is also warranted whenever houses or business places are nearby. Canvassing techniques are presented in Chapter 4.

Checklist Of Things To Do At The Scene

—*Fix the approximate collision site* with guidance from the client and information contained in the police accident report, if one was made (the report will often say, for example. "Place of accident approximately 2/10 mile south of the intersection of Goalby and Chrysler Avenues")

—*Closely examine the pavement surface* within a distance of 100 feet in both directions from where you think the collision occurred and across the entire pavement width. Look for gouging or scoring and debris consisting of loose dirt, fragments of rusted metal and, perhaps, shards of glass. These will likely indicate the precise point of impact (since debris has a tendency to splash like water, the center point should be considered the impact point). Examine the interior of any pavement gouges or scoring you find for signs of age. If the inside is clean and a different color than the surface, then the gouge is fresh and connected with your accident. But if it is dirty and the same color as the surface, it is probably old and not connected. *Photograph whatever marks or debris you find.*

—*Examine the pavement for skid marks* that may have been laid down by one or both cars. *Photograph and tape measure any marks you find.* If the police report refers to skid marks, do not accept the officer's measurements. There are many reasons for his error. He may have paced them off, measured hurriedly (it was a routine matter for him) or in fading light. The marks may be intermittent as the driver pumped his brakes and the officer failed to notice the continuation. Skid marks are valuable for two reasons; they can establish the speed and the path of the car that laid them.

—*When one or both cars are believed to have left the roadway* after impact, examine the berm, curbing, adjacent ground and standing objects (trees, shrubs, mailboxes, utility poles, fences) for tire or collision marks indicating where they exited the roadway and how far and what direction they travelled afterward. *Photograph all relevant markings you find.* This information will help you determine three things: the direction the car was travelling when it left the road, its speed and the degree of control or uncontrol over the vehicle which its driver had.

—*Photograph the roadway at the scene from all four compass points.* Take at least two shots in the direction your client was moving and two shots facing the opposite direction. One of each set of pictures should be at short range, showing the probable impact point from within 25 feet. The remaining pictures should be long range, from several hundred feet away, showing the contour, grade, any curves and dips in the road.

—*If view obstruction is claimed* by either driver (tree masking a stop sign; shrubbery blocking his view around a curve or corner; plants, weeds or building interfering with sighting down a railroad track, etc.) photograph the obstruction from the same approximate position in the road that the driver would have seen it. Hold the camera at roughly the same height as a driver's eyes (about 4 feet above the pavement). Assuming the photographs are taken before seasonal or physical changes have occurred, they will graphically support or refute the view obstruction claim.

Note: Whenever a seasonal change has altered foliage or natural growth conditions before you can photograph the scene, wait until those conditions are the same as at the time of the accident. . .if your case calendar permits the delay. Photographs of radically altered conditions are worthless. Of course, the delay is not warranted unless you believe the pictures will support your claim or refute that of your opponent.

—*Look for any road sign* (stop sign, warning sign, speed sign) or traffic signal (stop blinker, caution light, red and green intersection light) that is relevant to a liability issue in your case. Photograph it from the perspective of whichever driver was or should have been affected by it, by placing your camera in his lane facing the direction he travelled.

—*If an intersection traffic signal light is important* to your case, time the sequence of light changes. You may find a sudden change from green to red without an intermediate yellow. In one case I remember well, defense counsel discovered a simultaneous green condition for both intersecting streets over an interval of 5 seconds. He won his case on this evidence alone.

Note: Be sure to inquire of the road department that maintains the light whether any change in sequence or time intervals has occurred since the accident.

—*Prepare a detailed sketch of the accident scene* showing all conditions relevant to your case (relationship and direction of intersecting streets; location of landmarks, pavement marking, pavement gouge or scoring; location and length of skid marks etc.). Use a ruler for a uniform scale (1 inch= 20 feet is a good rule of thumb).

—Measure the width of the paved portion of the roadway, the width of each marked lane, width of both berms, the length of skid marks, the distance of debris or pavement scoring from the center line and the two pavement edges. Also measure the distance between the place where each vehicle came to rest and the point of impact, and from the resting place to the point at the pavement edge where either left the road. Measure the distance separating the approximate point of impact from the nearest standing landmark (i.e., utility pole, tree, fire hydrant, etc.) Enter all measurements on your sketch.

TWO IMPORTANT THINGS TO REMEMBER

1. *Be sure the client witnesses everything you do* at the scene, whatever finding and measurements you make and all photographs taken. Someone

may have to testify about each of these, if you do not settle the case, and that someone had better be him rather than you. It is an occasion to celebrate for the lawyer who has a fellow lawyer on the stand to cross-examine, because lawyers make extremely poor witnesses. They come on so strong, seem so cocksure and all-knowing, that jurors invariably discount their testimony by the very fact of their attitude, not to mention the obvious bias they carry to the stand.

2. *Write identifying and explanatory information for each photograph* you take in your note pad so that you remember later where the camera was held and the direction it pointed. *Do not write the information on the back of the print!* Some judges reject photographic exhibits bearing such writing. Even those who do not reject them out of hand require the information be obliterated.

GETTING TO THE BODY SHOP BEFORE
THE BODIES ARE REPAIRED OR DISMEMBERED

Homicides are sometimes solved by signs of injury the corpses bear. Not so in the case of violence to motor vehicles. Signs of injury rarely survive the death of a vehicle in an auto graveyard, where the corpse is invariably dismembered for its parts. Neither do the signs survive if death is avoided by repairing the damage, for new parts now replace the old and the vehicle emerges looking better than before.

So it is foolish to wait to evaluate vehcile damage until after the vehicle is repaired or cannibalized. The folly consists of important evidence lost.

Five Key Facts That Vehicle Damage Reveals

1. *Point of contact with the other vehicle or a stationary object.* The location of damage indicates the type of collision that occurred (whether front end, rear end, side-swipe or side angle blow). The existence of two separated damage sites evidences two separate impacts. The place of damage also tells much about the position of the vehicles at impact in relation to each other (e.g., substantial side damage that is localized suggests the front end of the other vehicle struck there).

2. *Point of contact with a pedestrian or cyclist.* Side damage supports the driver's claim that the pedestrian or cyclist ran into him. A dent indicates a solid blow, while a scrape or scratches indicate a glancing blow. A dent on top of the hood suggests the pedestrian came up and over the car,

while damage to the grill indicates he was probably carried forward by the car or thrown to either side.

3. *Degree of force applied to the other vehicle.* There is a direct correlation between the extent and location of damage and the force transmitted to the colliding object and its occupants. This is significant evidence supporting or refuting claims of injury in the other vehicle. Minor damage to soft structures (grill, headlights, door panels, side fender sections, trunk lid) evinces a minor impact and light force. But severe damage to sturdy structures (front and rear bumpers, frame posts, chassis) evinces a major impact and great force.

4. *Degree of force applied to your vehicle and its occupants.* The same correlation of damage and forces exist with respect to your client's vehicle, serving to corroborate or diminish your claims.

5. *Direction (vector) of forces applied to the vehicles and their occupants.* The location of vehicle damage also evidences the direction of forces that were transmitted to the occupants of the vehicles *and the necessary movement of their bodies in consequence.* Newton's laws of motion provide that for every action there is an equal and opposite reaction. Thus, if the damage to the adverse party's car is squarely in the rear, force was applied to his body from back to front. Reaction to the force would press him backward against his seat with an equal force, where, in theory, his body would remain. But in practice, his body would be flung forward because of new forces from inside the car which, in turn, obey the law. His seat reacts to his body force by forcing him forward. If he applies the brake after impact, the car slows but his body moves ahead at the same speed because of another branch of Newton's law dealing with momentum.

The practical significance of all this is that claims of injury caused by striking various portions of a car's interior can be supported or attacked by reference to the location of exterior damage. For example, if the only damage is squarely in the rear, it is physically impossible for the adverse driver to have been injured from contact with the passenger door. And if the only damage is squarely in the driver's door, it is highly unlikely his passenger could have injured his right side.

Here are some important techniques to follow in order to seize vehicle evidence before it vanishes.

Checklist of "Must" Steps To Find The Helpful Evidence

—As soon as you enter the case, locate all vehicles which were damaged in the accident. The police accident report will usually state whether they were driven away from the scene by their owners or towed away by a service truck. In the latter case, the report will often identify the body shop or storage yard to which it was towed. If the police report is not helpful, do the following:

1. *Phone the adverse party* (if not represented by counsel) and ask where his car was taken, whether repaired or not, who repaired it and, if not repaired, whether it will be and the body shop that will do the work. If his vehicle has already been repaired, ask the cost of same and portions of the vehicle that were damaged. Also ask him to mail you a copy of the repair bill. (The adverse party is likely to be cooperative at this non-suit stage since he hopes for an early settlement to avoid litigation and attorney fees.)

2. *If the adverse party is represented by counsel*, phone the latter for the same information and keep after him until you get it. Even after suit commences, counsel hopes for an early settlement and will accomodate you. Remember that your chief enemy in getting the information is delay, because of counsel's higher priority duties, or a tendency to procrastinate.

3. *If suit is pending* and opposing counsel refuses to volunteer the information, discover it via interrogatories or deposition of his client.

—Visit the body shops or storage yards where the damaged vehicles are located as quickly as possible after learning their whereabouts. Examine them minutely for damage, making detailed notes of the location and extent of damage. . .inside and out.

—Take photographs of the vehicles from all four sides, a sufficient distance away to show the entire side. Be sure that front and back views include the license plates for positive vehicle identification. Also take close-up photographs of damaged areas.

—Examine the interiors of the vehicles for evidence or damage caused by human body impact. Photograph the interiors whether damage is evident or not (pictures showing no interior damage vitiate from the adverse party's injury claims). Look for dried blood if lacerations are claimed.

—Check to see whether seat belts are installed in the vehicles (shoulder, lap or both) and whether the belts serving your client and the adverse party are operable. While all new cars are equipped, many older cars and other vehicles on the roads are without belts. There is a growing body of state case law holding that a jury may consider the fact that a plaintiff drove without a seat belt installed or buckled as evidence of contributory negligence (e.g. South Carolina) or as a basis for reducing recoverable damages (Texas).

—Draw rough diagrams of the vehicles showing the location and extent of damage. Also make a list of all damaged parts.

—Inspect the condition of the tires. If a tire is flat, the rim may have marked the pavement at the accident scene and you should reexamine the pavement for evidence of the precise place of impact. If one or more tires are bald, the vehicle's stopping capability was probably impaired and the condition may be admissible as evidence of owner negligence. *Photograph any flat or bald tire you find, whether on your client's vehicle or another* (it is as important to know and remember factors that adversely affect your case as those that benefit it).

—If any vehicle is at a body shop, ask the manager for a copy of any repair estimate he made and for names of other shops that estimated repair costs. Examine the estimate for damage items not visible to you (frame, motor or underside damage). If any vehicle is at a storage yard, ask the person in charge for names of all body shops that estimated repair costs.

—Phone all body shops that estimated repair costs on the adverse vehicle for the totals of their estimates. If any one total is significantly lower than the others, ask for a copy of that estimate (a measure of damages in the case of a repairable vehicle is the *reasonable* cost of repairing it, which is tantamount to the lowest cost at which adequate repairs are obtainable).

—If you learn that a vehicle has been repaired before you could view it, visit the shop that repaired it and obtain a copy of the repair bill properly itemized. Question the repairer about the nature, extent, and location of the damage as he observed it, whether any tire was flat or bald, whether there were operable safety harnesses, etc.

—*Important:* Always interview the tow truck driver that towed any vehicle from the scene. Ask him whether he saw debris on the pavement at the scene and, if so, obtain a description of it, its dimensions and location relative to the vehicles and the center line of the road. Also ask about the positions of the vehicles relative to each other and the roadway when he arrived at the scene. *Obtain a sketch or diagram of the scene from him, showing the location of vehicles and debris.*

Section B.   INVESTIGATING CRIMINAL CASES FOR DEFENSE PURPOSES

WHEN TO VISIT THE CRIME SCENE AND WHAT TO DO THERE

Visiting the scene can be as important to winning a criminal case as it is to winning a vehicle negligence case. But there is this difference between them. Whereas a visit is always indicated in accident cases, visiting a crime scene is only warranted in those classes of crimes where there is some chance of discovering helpful facts.

> **ACTION RULE:** Always visit the scene of the alleged crime unless by the nature of the crime charged, or the special circumstances of your case, you are certain there is no possibility of discovering a fact at the scene helpful to the defense.

Cases In Which A Scene Investigation Is Usually Warranted

The following partial list of common crimes admit of at least the possibility that a fact will be discovered at the scene that is valuable to the defense, because the scene is identified, can be readily located and is potentially important to the proof of some element of the charge:

arson	burglary
bribery	larceny
assault	robbery
murder	rape
manslaughter	riot
kidnapping	sale of drug or hallucinogen

Cases In Which A Scene Investigation Is Usually Not Warranted

There are unique classes of crimes which by their very nature militate against scene investigation, either because the scene is shifting, is indistinguishable or does not offer any hope of helpful facts. Here is a partial list that sufficiently identifies them:

crimes against public justice (e.g., perjury, escape from custody)	abandonment and neglect of children
crimes against government (e.g., treason, misprison)	obscene publications
libel and slander	forgery
crimes against family relation (bigamy, incest)	commercial and tax frauds
conspiracy	miscellaneous commercial (e.g., manufacture of unsafe products, blue sky violations)

The vast preponderance of felony prosecutions in state jurisdictions warrants visits to the scene because there is always a chance that something will be learned to defendant's advantage. You may find, for instance, that the physical surroundings preclude the possibility that your client committed the crime. The following burglary case exemplifies this possibility as well as good investigative technique by defense counsel.

ACTION EXAMPLE. . .A CRIME SCENE VISIT
THAT NETTED A CASE DISMISSAL

The owner of a small manufacturing plant came to work one morning to find that every desk drawer in the office had been forced and $150 in cash and postage stolen. Investigation disclosed that entry was gained through a rooftop ventilator, the cover of which was knocked aside.

Defendant was arrested and charged on the basis 1) that he was an ex-employee who had recently been fired, 2) that he had vowed to get revenge on his employer, 3) that when arrested, he had $100 he could not (or would not) account for, and 4) that he was seen near the plant the same night.

It was a strong circumstantial case for the State. Fortunately for defendant, his counsel knew the best way to beat a circumstantial case is to find another circumstance that breaks the incriminating syllogism (If A, B, and C are true, therefore D (guilt of defendant) must be true also).

Counsel found his circumstance on the building rooftop, by the simple expedient of going there with a yardstick and measuring the ventilator opening. It measured 18 inches, far too small to accomodate the defendant, who packed 175 pounds on a 5'8" frame. Counsel quickly arranged a demonstration with the prosecutor, at which defendant stripped to the buff, inserted both legs into the shaft, and promptly got stuck at thigh level. The charge was dismissed next day.

Once you have decided that your case warrants investigating at the scene, consider what physical fact or facts underlying the prosecution contentions are most vulnerable to attack (The identification of your client as the perpetrator, the means he used to gain entry to the building, or what he allegedly did after the crime). Then earmark those features for special attention at the scene (Was there enough light for an identification? Was it physically possible for defendant to gain entry that way? From what you observe at the scene, could defendant have acted that way afterward?).

Here is a list of techniques that will help you discover those favorable facts that are waiting to be found.

CHECKLIST OF THINGS TO DO AT THE SCENE

—*Visit the scene immediately after interviewing the defendant* and learning the prosecution claims (from the preliminary hearing or the prosecutor himself). If entry on private property is involved, phone the owner for permission to make sure it will be accessible. If he refuses permission, motion the court having jurisdiction of the case at this time (in felony cases, the municipal or comparable court has jurisdiction until bind-over to the grand jury; after bind-over, superior court or its comparable has it).

—*If the defendant is out on bail, take him with you to the scene.* He can help with any measuring and photographing you do and refresh his recollection of the scene. He can point out discrepancies between prosecution claims and his version of what happened (be sure to tell him not to speak about the case when another is within earshot). Finally, defendant's mere presence sometimes controls a complainant's tendency to exaggerate and substitute fancy for fact (see subsequent item).

—*Take the same equipment* that was recommended earlier for accident scene investigations. Also take your notes of the complainant's interview or preliminary hearing testimony and the prosecutor's contentions. Review the notes at the scene so you have in mind the precise claims you look to rebut as the investigation proceeds.

—*Examine all physical conditions* at the scene that are relevant to the case against defendant (e.g., precise location of the crime, its immediate surroundings and natural and artificial structures nearby). Determine whether the prosecutor's contentions about how the crime occurred and defendant's implication in it are consistent or inconsistent with such conditions.

—*Photograph the relevant physical conditions* whether or not you find inconsistency. At the very least, the photographs have value in helping you recall the scene later. Photograph the same condition from several positions according to your knowledge of witness location at the time of the event. Keep in mind that you may want to use the photographs as evidence, so be sure all prints are clear and recognizable. Write a description of each photograph (when and where taken and showing what) on your note pad and not on the back of the poloroid prints to preclude rejection of them as exhibits.

—*If the complainant is at the scene* (he may occupy the place where the crime occurred) ask him to show you what happened, besides telling you. Have him demonstrate the actions of defendant and himself.

    Caution: Be gentle but firm with complainants. Do not bully, but don't be obsequious either. "Would you mind demonstrating what happened?" often brings the answer, "Yes, I would mind." Request his cooperation with assurance, as though you have a right to interview him. . .which you do. . .and a right to his demonstration. . .which you do not.

—*Make a rough sketch of the scene* for future reference. Show the layout of the place, building or room with measured dimensions, location of doors and windows, location of artificial and natural structure, measured distances from nearest landmarks to the crime site and positions of the principals before, during and after the crime.

—*Measure the dimensions and distances* separating features of your sketch. Often you do not know at this stage how important distances may prove. In one murder case I remember, defendant claimed the deceased grabbed the rifle barrel and caused it to discharge. The prosecution never believed the claim, because defendant's statement said she stood in her kitchen pointing the gun at deceased who was in the bedroom, sitting on his bed. It seemed so absurd, the prosecutor never had the rooms measured nor even visited the house. Defense counsel did both and discovered that the kitchen and bedroom adjoined each other in the small house and had a common doorway, only 30 inches from the bed.

—*If the crime occurred at night* and defendant was identified at the scene, note all light sources in the vicinity (street lighting, sign lighting, auto traffic, etc.) and enter them on your sketch. Measure distances between the crime site and all light sources which could have assisted the identification. Make at least one visit to the scene at night at approximately the same time as the crime so you can perceive the extent of illumination. Be sure no lighting condition has changed since the crime by asking occupants nearby.

—*If the charge is burglary,* look for signs of forced entry onto the premises at the location and in the manner claimed by the prosecutor or complainant.

—*If the charge is rape,* look for signs of a struggle in the near vicinity (torn or uprooted plant growth if outside; torn or scratched upholstery if inside). If the scene is undisturbed, photograph it, even if months have elapsed since the event. It is always helpful evidence which, when coupled with prosecutors' common bias against such cases, often promotes a dismissal or reduced charge.

BUILDING A DEFENSE ON ALIBI

There is a true story about alibi told by lawyers in a midwestern city with as much relish today as when the event occurred 3 years ago. A defendant on trial for armed robbery was being cross-examined about his claim of alibi.

"Tell me," the prosecutor asked, "what do you understand the claim of 'alibi' to mean?"

Without giving his counsel time to object, defendant replied, "It means I was somewhere else when I did it."

Although counsel tried valiantly to explain the answer, the jury understood him well enough and disregarded the alibi witnesses, to convict.

Perhaps it is occurrences like this that leads so many defense counsel to ignore or half-heartedly pursue alibi opportunities. Whatever the reason, clearly the defense is not employed as often as it should.

> ACTION RULE: Whenever the defendant tells you he was not at the scene when the crime occurred and he is charged as the principal, prepare a defense based on alibi. Whether you believe him or not, your duty as his advocate requires your best effort to build a credible defense on that basis.

Having determined the defense is appropriate, how should you go about assembling evidence to support it? Start right away, for one thing. Procrastination is chronic among the losers of our profession; there is weak resistance to the impulse to put off until tomorrow the same work that was put off until today.

The best lawyers do resist. They understand that whenever proof of an issue depends on witness' testimony, the witnesses must be found and interviewed *now,* before their memories (or they themselves) disappear.

Here is a checklist of techniques that should be followed in preparing an alibi defense. They guarantee nothing except the strongest defense possible under your case circumstances.

Checklist For Preparing An Alibi Defense

—*Obtain a detailed chronological account* from the defendant of his activities during the period from at least four hours prior to four hours after the time when the crime occurred.

—*Go over each listed activity with* him carefully for the name and address of each person *who might have seen and recognized him.*

—*Review the list* of persons, places and times again with defendant for innaccuracies and inconsistencies (e.g., he couldn't have been at two places 10 miles apart within the space of 5 minutes). Cross-examine his recollection until you are satisfied you know all he knows.

—*If he does not know the name and address* of a potential alibi witness, learn everything else he knows about the witness (i.e., approximate age, size, appearance, voice, manner of speech, facial hair and any other distinctive personal characteristic.

—*Take a poloroid snapshot of defendant's face* for use in interviewing alibi witnesses, but only if his appearance is essentially unchanged from the day they saw him. If he has since shaved his beard or grown one, obtain an old photograph of him depicting the "before" image.

—Now selct from defendant's chronological account those activities, places and times which, if proved, preclude his guilt of the crime charged. (Preclude it because it would have been physically impossible for defendant to have committed the crime and been where he claims, due to the distance separating the two places and the time interval involved. *The witnesses defendant identifies at such places are crucial to a successful alibi defense.*

—*Interview these crucial witnesses yourself* wherever they can be found—as soon as possible after their identification. If defendant cannot identify one or more of them, go where he saw them and question people there and in the vicinity for names and addresses. Use the descriptions which defendant gave you previously.

—*If defendant is free on bail,* assign him the duty of interviewing the non-crucial but still important witnesses (i.e., persons who saw him some place other than the crime scene at a sufficient distance and time that it was possible for him to have travelled to the scene and committed the crime). While their testimony will never be decisive, it may be persuasive. . .especially if the place is far enough from the time near enough to and the activity incongruous with the place, time and manner of the crime.

—*Upon locating a prospective witness,* explain your case and mission before asking questions. Be sure he understands the importance to the defense of alibi verification; point out that if no person who saw defendant elsewhere at a critical time is willing to admit it, an innocent man will probably be convicted.

—*Next, tell the witness what defendant says concerning him* ("Bill tells me that on the night the crime is supposed to have occurred, Tuesday, June 6th, this year, he and you played pool together at the Variety Bar between 10 p.m. and midnight"). This is important not for the purpose of supplying a memory that does not exist, but to refresh a memory that does exist but is overlaid with others.

—*Finally, show him defendant's photograph* and ask if he remembers seeing defendant that night (not "did you see him", but "do you remember seeing him"—a different emphasis which is slight but significant).

—*If the witness denies seeing defendant* at the place you name, but admits being there that date and time, persist. Point out how unlikely it is that defendant would know he was there unless defendant saw him, and how likely it is that if defendant saw him, he must have seen defendant.

—*If the witness denies seeing defendant* and also denies being at the place that night. . .and he seems sincere. . .leave him and proceed to another prospect. If you think he is lying or merely mistaken, persist a while longer. Tell him he has nothing to fear by speaking out and that doing so will cost him nothing. Promise to reimburse any lost wages or expenses incident to any future discovery proceeding or court appearance. *But promise nothing more.* Purchased witnesses are defective case building tools . . .they always fail under stress.

—*Take a longhand, signed statement* from any witness who admits seeing defendant, detailing everything he remembers (date, time, location, what each did, what each wore and what each said). Include in the statement reasons why he remembers the date and defendant ("It was my bowling night and my teammates and I went to the bar to celebrate good scores. I remember playing pool with this fellow (client) for a couple of hours until I left around midnight. I won $5 from him.")

—Be sure to include personal information about the witness in his statement so you can locate him again when needed (i.e., residential and business addresses, employer, phone numbers, trade or profession, near relatives' names and addresses).

—*Ask him if he plans moving out of the area* in the near future. If he does plan a move or if he is unemployed, is a transient type or seems evasive about his plans, take his deposition as a material witness. While the deposition enables the prosecutor to cross-examine him, the risk that the witness will repudiate his admission or be impeached concerning it is better than the risk that he will not be available to testify when you need him.

—*In the extreme case* when an alibi witness is very favorable (his testimony will likely be decisive) he plans leaving the area soon and a deposition either cannot be obtained or will be much less effective than personal testimony, apply to the court for an order requiring him to post bail guaranteeing his appearance.

Filing The Notice Of Alibi

If your jurisdiction requires a written notice of alibi defense to be filed with the court, identifying the witnesses who will be called to establish it, file it immediately after completing your interviews. Get it on record before the pre-trial conference or plea bargaining session. Nothing much is gained by waiting until the deadline to file it and much can be lost. You may easily overlook the deadline date and be barred from introducing your evidence. Further, disclosing your alibi evidence early will sometimes produce a *nolle prosequi.* The prosecutor has time to check your witnesses out before having to prepare his case for trial. Then, realizing the merit of your defense, he will spare himself the effort of pursuing a probable defeat by shifting his energy to another case where victory is certain.

Should you wait until shortly before trial to file your notice, the prosecutor will likely have his case fully prepared and be unwilling to lose his investment of time and energy.

LOOKING FOR A CRIMINAL PAST OF THE CLIENT AND COMPLAINANT

Since the key witnesses in nearly every criminal case are the client and complainant, you cannot accurately evaluate your case until you have made an informed estimate of each one's credibility. . .the extent to which a jury is likely to believe what each says against the backdrop of available impeaching facts.

Few facts carry more impeachment weight than the fact of a prior felony conviction. Therefore, it is essential to your evaluation that you learn the state of the record for both principals, for the strength of your case is enhanced or impaired depending on whether the complainant or the client has the conviction record.

> **ACTION RULE:** Regarding the question of a criminal record, proceed on the assumption that a client can never be believed and a complainant can never be trusted. Check out all available sources of information no matter what your client says or how respectable the complainant appears.

A Typical Client Deception

Like the father of a pregnant teenager, defense counsel is often the last person to know about past transgressions. His client will freely admit cheating at cards or littering, but when it comes to admitting a prior felony conviction, his lips are sealed.

Not long ago, defense counsel interviewed his manslaughter client and asked whether he was ever convicted of a "serious" crime. Defendant answered negatively and counsel thought no more about it until the trial. To his dismay, the prosecutor introduced evidence of twelve prior felony convictions, ranging from burglary to pandering.

The jury added a thirteenth conviction. Counsel was furious at his client's deception. Pointing to his statement, he asked:

"Why did you tell me you never were convicted of a serious crime?"

"None of them *was* serious," defendant replied, ingenuously. "I never got more than a year for any of them."

Eight Sources For Information About Prior Convictions

1. *Defendant himself.* Ask him for details of *every* prior prosecution for crime, without regard whether it is a felony or misdemeanor and ended in a conviction. Demand information about every tangle with the law; date, place, accusation, police agency, his lawyer, courts in which he appeared and the disposition. Then, after getting his information, verify it by calling, visiting or writing the court and defense counsel that were involved.

2. *Complainant himself.* At the time you interview complainant, be sure to ask if he has ever been *arrested* for any crime, no matter how trivial he regards it. If he admits any, then get the same details as in the prior item and verify them in the same way. If complainant refuses to be interviewed and your jurisdiction allows discovery in criminal cases, take his deposition and ask the same questions there.

3. *The Prosecutor.* If defendant has a police record, the prosecutor probably knows of it from a F.B.I. fingerprint search. Ask him and you will abundantly receive. . .name, place, date, nature of crime and disposition. But you must ask!

   Caution: Do not assume that the prosecutor's information is accurate or that it relates to your client. There is vast room for errors in F.B.I. and state record check sheets the prosecutor draws from. Verify his information by personally examining court records. . .if the prosecution was local. . .and by writing or phoning the court if it was distant.

4. *Court records.* They serve a two-fold purpose; 1) to verify record information obtained elsewhere, and 2) as a source of original information. For the latter purpose, go to the Clerk's office of each court having jurisdiction over criminal prosecutions (i.e., municipal or recorder's court or their comparable; superior or common pleas court or their comparable). Examine the index of each criminal docket book (they are alphabetized) for entries pertaining to the client. Once having found an entry, go into the case docket book and case file for full details.

If the client and complainant lived an appreciable period at another location, write the clerks of court there for information. Be sure to enclose stamped, addressed envelopes for their use.

5. *Police records.* Most police departments in the country (all big city departments) preserve arrest records in alphabetical order for many years. This is especially true for felony arrests. Visit the record room of the department having jurisdiction where client and complainant live (county sheriff if the residence is outside an incorporated area). Ask the officer or clerk in charge to examine indexes for evidence relating to client and complainant. Although you can count on a few exceptions (defense lawyers are not held in deep esteem by police agencies) you will get their cooperation. Often enough to make the effort worthwhile, a hidden record will surface.

6. *Newspaper morgues.* All newspapers have clipping libraries containing stories of crimes and their sequelae (investigation, arrests, prosection) arranged alphabetically. Librarians are usually quite willing to search for helpful data. If either client or complainant ever was involved in a newsworthy crime (i.e., anything more serious than a traffic case) chances are good you can find out about it here.

7. *Relatives and neighbors.* If the client is closemouthed and evasive about his past history, his wife and other close relatives usually are not. Ask them about his past entanglements. If he is a young man, his parents should be questioned.

Neighbors are as good a source of information in criminal cases as in civil and subterfuge is not needed to obtain it. If the testimony of a complainant is essential to a conviction and he has lived at his current address an appreciable time, question his neighbors about any past police trouble. If he has had it, they know about it. Among any five neighbors a man has, at least one can be counted on to disclose the facts.

8. *Business competitors.* As no one knows the demerits of a doctor better than another doctor, so no one knows more about the skeleton in the closet of the businessman-complainant than his competitor. If your case involves an alleged burglary, robbery, theft or embezzlement from a business establishment, question complainant's competitors about his reputation for honesty. You may find reasons to believe the crime never occurred or is exaggerated. Insurance and bond coverages are sometimes irresistable plums to financially-troubled or larcenous businessmen. And once one plum has been safely digested, another seems even more enticing. The pattern of fraud is set and your client may be caught up in its design. Information from competitors may reveal the pattern and provide you with strong impeachment. Better yet, your information

disclosed to the prosecutor may prompt a dismissal, as he sees how hollow a foundation his case rests upon.

Action Example—How Counsel Discovered A Business Fraud And Freed His Client

I remember a burglary case in which defendant was arrested and charged on circumstantial evidence with having entered a jewelry store through the skylight and stolen a dozen pieces of expensive jewelry.

Defense counsel questioned four local jewelers and discovered that while the complainant had experienced three burglaries in the past two years, *none of the others had been burglarized at all.* Counsel went to complainant's insurance company with his information and the latter went to the police.

The investigation was re-opened on the pretext of gathering added evidence against the client. Within days police discovered, 1) the skylight had been broken from the inside, and 2) the jewelry was hidden in an empty paint can in the basement.

MAKING THE BEST USE OF PRELIMINARY HEARINGS AS FACT SOURCES

One of the most valuable of all pre-trial opportunities for the defense is the preliminary hearing, the occasion when a magistrate determines whether there is enough evidence against the accused to warrant sending him to superior court (common pleas, in some states) for grand jury action or trial.

Three Rewards To Win From Pre-Trial Hearings

The preliminary hearing comes early in the case against the accused, often before his counsel has more than begun his investigation. This timing, coupled with the hearing's procedure and purpose, presents the possibility of three rewards to the lawyer who sees its value:

1. *The hearing can result in a case dismissal.* If the magistrate decides that insufficient evidence has been presented to make a prima facie showing that a crime was committed or that defendant committed it, he must dismiss.
2. *It gives counsel a chance to build important impeachment bases* against prosecution witnesses. The prosecutor has the burden of making a prima

facie showing. Defense counsel has no burden. The prosecutor must present witnesses to satisfy his burden. Defense counsel need present no one...and if he presents no witness, only he has the right of cross-examination. Such an advantage! By detailed and searching cross-examination, you can freeze the story of each prosecution witness...at a time when he is, probably, inadequately prepared. Any future change of story creates a blistering impeachment opportunity.

3. *Counsel can learn the essential facts that serve as the cornerstones of the prosecution case.* When and where the alleged crime occurred, what it consists of, how it happened, how defendant was implicated, who else is involved, who discovered it, what was discovered, what policemen investigated, what they did, what they found, etc. Counsel sees the strengths of the prosecution case and may, perhaps, perceive its weaknesses. Facts he learns and identities discovered at the hearing always aid his investigation. The first tell him what he must verify or refute, the second, who he must question or contradict.

Waiving The Hearing Is Waving Goodbye To Opportunity

After such a recital of advantage, why should defense counsel ever want to waive preliminary hearing? Yet waive it they do in vast numbers, in every jurisdiction and before every magistrate. Unconscious of the opportunity lost or unheeding whether it be lost or won.

> ACTION RULE: Always attend a preliminary hearing and never agree to waive it, no matter how inconvenient the attendance is or how accommodating to prosecutor and magistrate the waiver will be.

Checklist Of Seven Steps To Take At The Preliminary Hearing

1. *Make certain a court reporter is in attendance* to record the testimony. Find out in advance if the court will supply one. If not, hire an independent reporter on your own. If you represent an indigent defendant, the court will usually authorize payment out of court funds or assess it as a part of costs.
2. *Cross-examine each prosecution witness* in detail and at length. Do not limit your examination to the subjects covered on direct, but explore every nook and cranny of witness knowledge that is relevant to any issue of your case.
3. *Give each witness full rein to answer and the prosecutor every license to question on direct.* Do not object to any question or answer because it

violates an evidentiary rule. This is not the trial and waiving objections will not hurt you. But making them may hurt you. Information from prosecution witnesses is what you want, the more the better. Objections that are sustained are like gags, stifling facts that may be used to your advantage later on.

4. *Make copious notes* of witness testimony and take all the time that is necessary to do so. Interrupt the prosecutor's questioning whenever you fall behind so you miss nothing important. Only explain your trouble courteously and even the testiest judge will show patience. Even if he is the exception, better you should lose his patience than lose your facts.

5. *Obtain reports from police witnesses* that they used to refresh their recollections before testifying. If you establish that use during cross-examination, many judges will permit you to see the reports. . .to test how accurately the testimony reflects the source. Once you have the documents, examine them closely for helpful facts and witness names unknown before. Again, take all the time you need. Ask the judge for a short recess if several pages must be read.

6. *If there are prosecution witnesses present at the hearing who were not called to the stand for the State,* call them to the stand for defendant. Question them exhaustively on direct examination. You are not bound at the trial to whatever they say here. Moreover, the fact they were not called may mean they have important facts to contribute, but the prosecutor plans to hold their contribution in reserve. . .as a surprise. . . until needed. Calling these reserves as your witnesses is the kind of unorthodox, hence unexpected, technique that unsettles opposition and produces settlements.

7. *Resist a finding of prima facie showing by the magistrate when the prosecutor rests his evidence.* Do not concede it even when obvious to you. It may not be obvious to the judge. Your opposition may not result in a dismissal, but it may force the prosecutor to introduce more evidence. *Remember:* your interest lies in forcing him to reveal as much of his case facts as possible, so you can assess his strengths, detect his weaknesses and discover leads to profitable evidence.

FINDING THE CONSTITUTIONAL VIOLATION THAT LEADS TO SETTLEMENT OR ACQUITTAL

"Most prosecutors are like grade school bullies," a veteran defense lawyer once remarked. "They like to fight when they're certain to win and like to negotiate everything else." It is a trait of all lawyers. . .certainly not limited to prosecutors. . .to want to try our certain victories and settle our possible defeats. But the trait is more noticeable in prosecutors. Their disposition to settle in the face of any opposing strength stems from necessity, not cowardice. The vast number of cases at any moment, contrasted with the meager judicial and prosecutor manpower, makes plea-bargained settlements an utter necessity to prevent a total collapse of the system.

Now add the pressure from due process, the constitutional demand that all criminal trials be speedy, and the reasons are apparent why your opponent seizes any justification for advancing a reduced charge or nolle request. *Your job as defense counsel is to provide him that justification, a weakness in his case that shows him victory is not certain.*

Why A Constitutional Weakness Is As Good As A Merit Weakness

Decision by technicality has been deplored by layman and legal philosopher alike. But, of course, neither is in charge of court business. In the area of criminal law, never in history have so many "technical" opportunities been available to defense counsel as now. Under the guidance of the Warren court, innumerable roadblocks have been put in prosecutors paths, consisting of constitutionally defective police procedures, news media excesses and expanded rights of accuseds.

Your may not think them technicalities at all, but substantive principles. Or you may believe they threaten disorder. But whatever you believe, whether you agree or disagree, know and act upon this. Your duty to your client requires that you create and exploit the opportunities.

> ACTION RULE: Always investigate police procedures used in your case to obtain prosecution evidence, having in mind the procedures which the Federal Supreme Court has decreed must be followed. Any violation of the second by the first constitutes a positive factor in your case evaluation and may be a basis for settlement negotiation and a pre-trial motion to suppress.

CREATIVE DEFENSIVE OPPORTUNITIES

Here are some frequently used police and prosecution procedures that violate constitutional standards often enough to merit your close attention whenever one or more surfaces in your case. The citations are to landmark Supreme Court cases establishing the respective standard.

Checklist Of Constitutional Violations To Look For

—*Seizure of physical evidence without a search warrant pursuant to an illegal arrest.* Police may search and seize evidence in your client's possession subsequent to a *valid* arrest. If the arrest is invalid, the evidence may be suppressed upon your motion to the court having jurisdiction of the pending case. Most arrests are made without an arrest warrant. For a warrantless arrest to be valid, the arresting officer must have probable cause to believe a crime was committed *and* that your client committed it. *Mapp v Ohio, 367 US 643.*

Learn the circumstances surrounding his arrest from the client and the facts that were known to the arresting officer at the time. Obtain the latter information at the preliminary hearing, by deposing him, or by examining him at the hearing of your motion to suppress.

—*Seizure of physical evidence pursuant to a search warrant not based on probable cause.* Get client's copy of the search warrant from him. Next, examine the affidavit of the police officer who obtained the warrant. The affidavit is a statement of facts known to the officer. The facts must be sufficient to establish *probable cause* for the belief that a crime has occurred and that specified evidence relevant to it is in your client's possession at the specified place. The affidavit must contain facts, not rumors, suspicions, or surmises. *Spinelli v United States, 393 US 410.*

You can usually determine quite accurately from a reading of the affidavit whether the "probable cause" standard has been met, or whether the seizure was illegal and the evidence subject to your motion.

> **A RULE OF THUMB THAT JUDGES USE: Ask yourself this question.** Assuming all facts stated in the affidavit are true, is it probable (not possible) that the named crime was committed and the named evidence relating to it can be found now in accused's possession?
>
> If you answer "yes", so will the judge who hears your motion. If the answer is "no", the judge may also answer negatively, and you have a strong constitutional argument.

—*A confession or inculpatory statement was obtained from your client after arrest and before arraignment and the time interval between them was unnecessarily long.* The case of *Mallory v United States, 384 US 436,* lays down the rule that an accused must be brought before an arraigning magistrate without unnecessary delay after his arrest, so that bond may be set, his rights explained, and counsel secured. If the time interval is longer than the judge who hears your motion thinks necessary under the circumstances (e.g., 48 hours has been held too long a delay without proof of necessity) and a confession or damaging statement taken from the client during the interim, the statement should be suppressed.

Learn the time interval from defendant and the circumstances showing necessity, or lack of it, from police officers at the preliminary hearing, on depositions, or at the hearing on your motion.

—*A confession or inculpatory statement was obtained from your client without his having been told his "Miranda" rights. Miranda v Arizona, 384 US 436,* provides that before a statement can be obtained from an accused after his arrest that is admissible in court, he must be told the following: that he has the right to remain silent; that whatever he says may be used against him; that he is entitled to the presence of his lawyer during the questioning, and, that if he is indigent and wants a lawyer, one will be supplied him at no cost.

If the prosecutor relies on a confession or damaging statement, find out from your client what warning he was given and when (it must be reasonably soon before the questioning). Cross-examine the interrogating officers at the preliminary hearing, on deposition or at the hearing on your motion to suppress. While most all will have memorized the Miranda litany, there are enough slip-ups to make your effort worthwhile.

—*Your client was identified at a line-up without you having been notified it was scheduled and given a chance to attend.* A line-up after a formal charge is placed as a critical stage of the prosecution case and an accused's counsel must be notified in time to attend if he is known. If no counsel has yet been retained, the accused must be told he has a right to counsel's presence, given a chance to call one in and, if he is indigent, told a lawyer will be supplied him without cost upon request. *Rivers v United States 3 Crim Law Reports 3263.*

If the client participated in a line-up, ask him to describe the other men in the line (they must be reasonably similar in description; (not all black if he is white or all white if he is black) and to tell you what he was told about his rights. Examine police participants at the preliminary hearing, on deposition or at the hearing of your motion to suppress the out-of-court identification.

—*Evidence was obtained against defendant through the use of a wiretap of his phone or from an overheard conversation involving himself.* If an illegal wiretap or illegally-overheard conversation led to evidence which resulted in defendant's prosecution, the evidence may be suppressed on motion *(Alderman v United States, 394 US 165).* Whenever you suspect either one (your client suspects it or tells you it is the only way police could have been led to the evidence) examine every police officer connected with the investigation about the subject. Once you discover the existence of either the wire tap or an overheard conversation and that it was illegal (research the laws governing in your jurisdiction) the Alderman case provides that you are entitled to a turnover of all transcripts made by police. From these and further examination of the officers. . .at a special court hearing for the purpose. . .you can determine whether the conversation led to the evidence.

The Permanency Of Procedural Rights

There is a tendency among some criminal defense counsel to soft-pedal these and similar procedural opportunities today, apparently on the assumption that the demise of the "Warren court" means the demise of the rigid police standards they espoused. Not so. *Stare decisis* has always had a greater impact on criminal law than the changing of the court guard. Especially so in the context of procedural rights for those accused of serious crime.

Like legislators originating new taxes, judicial inventors of new rights may come and go, but their handiwork always survives them. So, get acquainted with the defensive opportunities these rights afford you. They will become old friends and allies.

6

How To Take Statements That Promote Settlement And Trial Success

TABLE OF CONTENTS

6

How To Take Statements That Promote Settlement And Trial Success

"To Write With Ease Is A Sign Of Breeding,
But Easy Writing Is Cursed Hard Reading."
Alexander Pope

A well-written statement is many things of value to a lawyer. It is a diary, preserving the recollections of the client for future refreshment. It is a treasure chest, holding invaluable facts supplied by friendly or disinterested witnesses. It is a scabbard, holding a slashing impeachment against an unfriendly witness. Whenever it is any one of these, it is also a lever, moving a reluctant opponent toward settlement.

A very able trial lawyer once told me that he could accurately guage the ability of his opponent by the condition of his witness statements.

"If he has no statements, or very few, I consider him careless, lazy, inexperienced or professionally ignorant," he said. "If he has statements from most of the important witnesses, I consider him just the opposite.
"And if he has the statements and they all say something that helps his case, I consider settling."

This chapter offers techniques for getting statements from your important witnesses, ensuring that they say something benefitting your case and say it as clearly and effectively as possible. It considers and compares the three statement media, writing, shorthand or stenotype reporting and tape recording. It discusses the different purposes of statements from the different classes of witness, friendly, unfriendly and disinterested and shows you how to achieve those purposes.

Finally, the chapter tells you how to authenticate the statement of a witness who refuses to sign it, so its validity can never be questioned.

Section A: GENERAL GUIDELINES FOR STATEMENTIZING

SIX QUESTIONS EVERY WITNESS
STATEMENT SHOULD ANSWER

Journalists succeed where most lawyers fail. . .in the art of writing effectively. Examine a front page story in any daily newspaper and marvel at the art displayed. It flows so smoothly that it seems effortless. Far from it. The easier the reading, the harder the writing.

Although the construction of a news story bespeaks art, it also bespeaks an understanding of the purpose of the article, *which is to inform*. A witness statement is no different in its purpose.

> **ACTION RULE:** The general purpose of every witness statement is to inform you, a witness, your opponent, a judge or jury about facts that are relevant to your case or relate to the maker. Words that fail either test do not belong there.

To make certain each statement you write contains all the necessary information, use the same key word outline that journalists use. . .who, when, where, what, how and why. . .and see that each is answered in the statement.

Checklist Of Key Word Questions

1. *Who?*. . .Who is giving the statement? Identify him by full name, address and telephone number. Who is referred to in the statement, is involved in the event the statement describes? State his, her or their full names, addresses and telephone numbers, if known.
2. *When?*. . .When did the event(s) occur? State the precise day, date and time, if known. If only an approximation can be made, say so. Do not omit the information, because it may be important even if approximate. If a precise date is crucial to your case (e.g., statute of limitations and alibi defenses) and the witness supplies it, explain in the statement how he recalls it. The witness will be more confident of the accuracy of the information later on. Also, the explanation enhances his credibility. When was this statement taken? State the day, date, and hour. This information adds to the statement's appearance of authenticity and is especially valuable in case the witness denies making the statement. He must now lie about his whereabouts at the time.

3. *Where?*...Where did the event(s) occur? Describe and identify the location as precisely as is possible to the witness (i.e., do not say, if you can help it, "The collision occurred at the intersection of Linda Vista and Morena Streets." Instead say if you can, "The collision occurred in the northwesterly quarter ("quadrant" would sound like a lawyer, not a witness) of the intersection of Linda Vista and Morena Streets, about 15 feet south of the Morena Street crosswalk.")

   If the witness is not sure of the exact location, say so ("The collision occurred somewhere in the intersection of Linda Vista and Morena Streets, I'm not sure just where.").

   Where is this statement given? State the room, building and address as an aid to statement authenticity.

4. *What?*...What happened? What is the event(s) all about? What did each participant do or say? If the description is favorable to you, also describe the witness' location at the time. Explain how and why he was able to perceive what he describes.

   If the description of events is unfavorable, explain any condition that militates against witness perception (e.g., it was night and the scene was dark...the witness was 150 feet from speaker when an admission was made).

   If the description is unfavorable and the witness admits any uncertainty, express it in the statement ("I am not completely certain this is what happened, but I think so. It was a long time ago.")

5. *How?*...How did the event(s) happen? What forces or agencies were involved? ("The left front end of the Chrysler came over the center line and struck the left side of the Ford"..."They were fighting and Bob hit Sid with his fist, knocking him to the ground. As he fell, Sid's head struck a flagstone hard.")

   What was the quality of the act, suggesting a state of mind? ("He wasn't looking where he was driving, but was looking back at his passenger"..."I told him I wanted something to clean up grease with and he sold me the product, saying it was safe and effective. He never told me it might burn my skin",)

6. *Why?*...Why did the event(s) happen? What was the efficient or producing cause? What reason was expressed by the actor? ("He was driving too fast and too close to the car ahead, so when it stopped, he couldn't stop in time"..."He said he was sick and tired of me nagging him about his drinking, then he slapped me.")

   If the witness opinion is unfavorable and he has no facts to support it, say so. ("I didn't see the car long enough to say how fast it was going, but I'm sure it was going too fast.") If the witness opinion is favorable, be sure to state the facts on which it is based. (e.g., "I was going about 50 m.p.h. and he passed me like I was standing still.")

WHAT MEDIUM TO USE. . .PAPER, REPORTER OR RECORDER

There are three forms a witness statement may take and it is difficult to compare them. They perform different functions and respond to different needs. A handwritten or typewritten statement prepared by the lawyer or his investigator—a statement taken down in shorthand or stenotype by an official or independent court reporter—or a statement recorded on tape; there is no "best" among them, only a "better" sometimes in certain situations. Here are some standard situations when one or another medium should be used.

When A Handwritten Or Typewritten Statement Should Be Taken

1. *Whenever a a friendly witness other than the client, has been interviewed*, not including the client. The latter is completely under your control, hence no formal memorial of his facts is necessary to ensure future conformity.
2. *Whenever a disinterested witness is interviewed and expresses no objection to such statement.* You have no control over him whatsoever, but depend entirely upon such good will as you can engender. Putting his words in statement form over his objection risks alienating him, a far greater injury than the benefit of the statement.
3. *Whenever an unfriendly witness is interviewed and you have time to write a statement* of what he says. Do write it after you obtain his facts, even if he says he will not sign it. Techniques for getting his authentication without getting his signature are presented later in this chapter.

When A Court Reporter Shorthand Or Stenotype Statement Should Be Taken

1. *Whenever a disinterested witness whose testimony is likely to be vital to your case is interviewed.* Take a court reporter along as insurance against the possibility the witness may object to a handwritten statement, give you insufficient time to write it or balk at authenticating it. If no obstacle arises, by all means write up your own statement in addition to the reporter statement. You may decide to save the expense of

transcribing the latter and you only have the option if you also have your statement.

2. *Whenever an unfriendly witness is interviewed* (adverse party included) unless you are positive his testimony will not be important. . .for or against you (such as a police witness whose only connection with the case is as custodian of public records).

   Note: If the witness was in a position to know something significant about the issues of your case (e.g., a passenger in the adverse party's car, a member of the police investigating team, or the adverse party's agent having some role in the transaction) take a court reporter with you to his interview. Even if you learned from another source that he "knows" nothing helpful or hurtful, take the reporter to record that he "knows nothing." A negative statement bars the later recollection that can suddenly occur—or supplies you with impeachment ammunition if it is asserted.

When A Tape Recorded Statement Should Be Taken

1. *Whenever a friendly witness is interviewed,* including the client. Make a tape in addition to your written statement. It guards against future loss or misplacement of the statement, is cheaper and more accurate than having your secretary take it in shorthand and is easily stored for future review and possible transcription. Be sure to test the equipment before the interview for voice level. Then, continue testing the level periodically throughout the interview by playing back 10-15 second segments (I remember a case in which defense counsel at a divorce pre-trial conference claimed to have taped serious admissions of plaintiff. When the tape was played, however, all that was heard was whispering noises, like wind through a willow tree).

2. *Whenever a disinterested witness is interviewed and expresses consent* to a recording. Be sure to have him state his consent at the very beginning of the recording and again at the end.

3. *Whenever an unfriendly witness is interviewed and the client cannot afford the cost of a court reporter,* or no reporter is available. (*Remember,* if you represent plaintiff, the Code of Ethics permits you to advance this cost as long as both you and the client understand you are to be reimbursed out of any recovery.)

   While the chances of getting consent to a recording may be only fair, I know lawyers who have succeeded repeatedly. You should make the effort.

Three Further Considerations About Statement Media

1. *Court reporters are expensive,* especially in metropolitan areas where an hourly charge of $25-$30—including travel time and mileage is commonplace. Be sure to ask the rate before you hire him and then pay the bill promptly upon receipt.

   Challenging his fee after the interview or procrastinating on payment can lose the benefit from a potent statement. Disgruntled reporters have been known to delay transcribing statements until too late for settlement or trial use. (In one instance of a seriously impeaching statement, a reporter whose bill was unpaid had to be subpoenad to the trial with his transcript. Then the lawyer discovered that the contradiction he was counting on was missing from the transcript. The reporter was all innocence and rectitude and the judge decided the lawyer's notes rather than the transcript erred. The lawyer left the courtroom, chagrined—and the reporter left having made his point.

2. *A shorthand reporter is better than a stenotype reporter for the purpose of statement-taking.* The first is far less obtrusive than the second, tending to merge with the background after introductions. The stenotype machine is an unfamiliar gadget which often seems to preoccupy a witness. In the case of an unfriendly witness, the difference in reporters is sometimes the difference between getting and not getting an interview.

   If you have a choice, then, opt for the shorthand reporter. Many independent firms have at least one on its staff, but you must ask for her.

3. *If you represent defendant in an insurance covered case,* ask the insurance adjuster for copies of all written statements he took from the adverse party and/or other witnesses. Also ask him for transcripts of telephonic taped statements. (Some of the large casualty insurers with staff adjusters take tape recorded statements by telephone, routinely.)

   Note: Do not forego taking your own statements merely because your insurance company took its own. If you are forced to use the latter during trial, not only the fact of insurance, but the identity of the insurer are disclosed to the jury.

TECHNIQUES OF EFFECTIVE STATEMENT WRITING

The most important rule of statement writing also applies to every form of legal writing, but is more crucial in the case of statements than elsewhere:

ACTION RULE: Prepare the statement carefully in your mind before beginning to write. Determine in advance which facts the witness supplied you will use and in which order, which you will highlight by repetition and which you will subordinate by glossing over. Be conscious of the class of witness he belongs to and the purposes to be achieved by his statement. Then, determine how best to achieve those purposes and begin to write, applying proper writing techniques checklisted here.

The *sine qua non* of this rule—and the element most violated in practice—is the requirement of preparation. It requires a discipline which too many lawyers lack, to wait while the witness watches, pen poised but not busy, while the mind sorts and evaluates facts in the light of objectives; fashioning the statement mentally before fashioning it verbally.

Every lawyer should have Pope's maxim tattooed in his brain:

If you think twice before you write once, you will write twice the better for it.

Once the evaluation process is done and the statement is visualized, write the statement using the following techniques.

Checklist Of Writing Techniques

—*Complete your interview before starting to write the statement.* Review the questions asked and answered first, to be sure every significant question has been covered.

—*Make notes of significant facts* (relevant directly or indirectly to any issue of your case) stated by the witness. Unless your time or his is limited, take sufficient time between each question to permit accurate and complete notes.

—*Use lined statement paper* with two carbon copies (one copy for a friendly or disinterested witness and one file copy). Statement sets with carbon inserts may be purchased at most legal form stores.

—*Write on a firm, smooth surface*—a table top or a clipboard. If you are in a witness' home without a clipboard, ask to use his kitchen or dining room table.

—*Write the day, date, time and location of the interview and the name of the interviewee* at the upper right hand corner of page one. In this location the statement is quickly identified. And the prominence and primacy of the data insures against omission.

—*From your interview notes, choose the facts that best achieved* the purposes of the statement. (The purposes of a friendly, unfriendly and disinterested witness statement will be discussed later in this chapter.)

—*Write legibly* so that anyone besides you can read and understand it. If your handwriting resembles Sanskrit, print. Better yet, buy a used, portable typewriter and take it with you to witness interviews.

—*Use the witness' words as much as possible* rather than your own. If he said, "The car speeded up, crashed the light, and struck me," write it that way. Don't write, "The car accelerated, violated the traffic signal light and collided with my car."

Note: But if the witness' words innacurately express his meaning, then substitute your own, retaining his vernacular. For example, if he said, "Rose hit Bennett and missed," he may mean either Rose hit *at* Bennett and missed, or Rose hit Bennett and missed what he was aiming at. . .his nose. Find out his meaning, then express it clearly.

—*Write short, simple sentences and break paragraphs frequently.* The statement is meant to be easily read and understood. Non-stop sentences filled with subordinate clauses and interminable paragraphs filling the page with black ink obstruct understanding as surely as if you wrote partly in a foreign language.

—*Use the first person singular* as though it was the witness writing. This tense is personal and authentic. Using the third person, on the other hand, produces a stilted, awkward, impersonal, and secondhand statement that is much less effective.

—*Do not clean up the witness' grammar or language.* If he tells you, "I seed him look the other way, then he come into the road and popped me," write it that way. Don't write, "I saw him look the other way, then he drove into the road and collided with my car." You must strive for maximum authenticity and you always lose some of it when you lose the flavor of his speech. If you write it your way, when he answers you from the witness stand, "I never said that!" he is absolutely right.

Section B.   STATEMENTIZING THE CLIENT AND FRIENDLY WITNESS

UNDERSTANDING THE PURPOSES OF THE STATEMENT

Because a written statement is taken from both friendly and unfriendly witnesses, many lawyers seem to believe the same techniques are involved. . . to achieve the same purposes. Not so. While there are obvious similarities (e.g., both record witness recollections) there also significant differences.

Chief among the differences is the use to which each statement will be put because one is from an ally and the other is from an enemy. The first embodies and emphasizes facts that promote your case and is used to build your evidence for settlement or trial. The unfriendly witness statement, on the other hand, should contain facts inconsistent with or contradictory to facts known to you, other facts in the same statement, or other facts you expect an adverse witness to assert at trial. Its primary use, therefore, is to damage your opponent's evidence by impeaching his witnesses.

> **ACTION RULE: Every statement should be designed to reflect the status of the witness whose statement it is, achieve the purposes for which you want it and advance the use to which it will be put.**

Before discussing techniques that should be used in writing up the statement of the client or a friendly witness, first examine the purposes of the statement that writing techniques must achieve.

Six Purposes Of The Client And Friendly Witness Statement

1. *As a record of all significant and relevant facts pertaining to your case that is known to the witness, made at the time when his memory of them is fresh.*
2. *As a means of refreshing your memory of the facts during the pendancy of the case.*
3. *As a means of refreshing the witness' memory of the facts during the pendancy of the case—to prepare him to answer interrogatories or questions at an oral deposition.*
4. *As a sounding board of favorable facts, selected and emphasized to present the most potent version of your case.*
5. *As a means of preparing the witness to testify during trial.*
6. *As a settlement lever embodying a strength in your case, favorable facts told by one who is prepared to repeat them in court.*

HOW TO WRITE UP THE STATEMENT OF THE FRIEND

Mindful of the general writing techniques listed earlier and the purposes served by the statement of your client or witness, consider now the content of the statement. What facts should be included and what facts omitted? In what sequence should included facts be presented? Should they be presented uniformly or should certain facts be emphasized? And if the latter, how emphasize them?

ACTION RULE: A client or friendly witness statement should exemplify putting your best case foot forward. Since the statement will be used to persuade your opponent to settle and to prepare the witness for discovery and trial testimony if the persuasion fails, it should contain only strength. Only favorable facts relating to the issues of your case should be included. Make a separate record of any unfavorable facts learned during the interview. Clip it to your copy of the statement so it can be easily detached when the latter is given to your opponent to read.

Checklist Of What To Do To Produce A Strong Statement

—Write or type up the statement in your office immediately following the interview and in the presence of the client or witness.

—From your completed witness checklist form and other interview notes, identify facts that are relevant to some issue of your case. Place a number next to each such fact statement, numbering in succession according to the order in which you want the facts placed in the statement. *(In general, statement facts should answer the "six key questions" in this order...who, when, where, what, how, and why)*

—From the facts so identified and numbered, distinguish between those which are favorable to your case and those facts which are unfavorable.

—Now write or type the statement, *excluding the unfavorable facts,* so it presents the following information in narrative form:

　　1. Identity and address of the witness and statement date.
　　2. Facts establishing a foundation for the witness. (where he was, and when, what he did, and what he perceived)
　　3. Favorable facts relevant to one or more of your claims or defenses.

　　Remember: A statement is meant to be an edited interview result and not the entire result itself. Don't include everything the witness said even if it is relevant and favorable. To do so is to lose your bearings in a blizzard of words and bleed impact from his "best" facts.

—*Highlight the specially significant favorable facts by repeating them.* If the witness says the adverse party struck your client without provocation by word or act; drove into the intersection without stopping for the stop sign; admitted being the owner of the dog that did the biting, etc., write the fact twice at different places in the statement. "What's worth knowing once is worth stating twice."

—Whenever the witness is imprecise about a favorable fact, speaks in generalities or estimates over a range of values, construe it most liberally in your favor. Write down the most favorable specific or value encompassed by the generality or fitting in the range. (If the witness says the adverse party "appeared to be intoxicated after the accident," write that he was "drunk." If he says the party was driving "anywhere from 60 to 80 miles per hour," write that he was driving "80 miles per hour.")

—Give the client or witness a copy of the statement. Ask him to keep it in a safe place and to read it over from time to time to renew his recollections.

—Whenever the witness' facts describe a scene or refer to an event occurring at a scene (accident or crime scene and the event that occurred there; location and extent of real or personal property damage) make a diagram on a separate page of the statement referring to and consistent with his statement facts. This depiction of facts is quite effective in "selling" them to your opponent and as a reminder to the witness months later.

—Have the witness sign both the statement and diagram, after writing the appropriate following paragraphs in his own hand:

"I have read this   page statement and it is true."
"I have examined this diagram and it is accurate."

In addition, get his signature or initials at the bottom of each page of a multi-page statement. Although there is little danger that he will repudiate his statement or diagram. . .unlike the unfriendly witness. . .signatures are important for another reason. They convey an authenticity to your opponent during settlement discussion that is altogether missing in their absence.

ACTION EXAMPLES: A FRIENDLY WITNESS INTERVIEW AND STATEMENT

Here is a listing of facts obtained from a friendly witness in a motor vehicle negligence case, followed by the actual statement the lawyer prepared. Notice how he employs several techniques contained in the preceding checklist to produce a clear, readable, and strong statement. See if you can tell which side this lawyer represents from his handling of facts in the statement.

Summary Of Facts Obtained During Interview With Mary Campana

—52 years old, married to John. . .lives at 1632 Canterbury Rd., Cleveland, with husband, 2 sons, Harold and Kenneth.

—Riding as sole passenger of 1968 Plymouth 2 door Sedan, owned and driven by Reba Calhoon, 1628 Canterbury Rd., Cleveland. . .involved in 2 car accident approx. 2 p.m., Monday, December 21, 1970, at intersection of E. 185th Street and Lake Shore Blvd., Euclid, O.

—Riding next to driver in front seat. . .coming from style show/luncheon at Statler Hilton Hotel, Euclid Ave. . .*just driving around before going home.*

—Eastbound on Lake Shore Blvd approx. *30-40 m.p.h.* as approached intersection. . .car in inside lane of 2 lanes eastbound. . .she and Mrs. Calhoon talking about dresses displayed at show. . .*Calhoon looked at her frequently ("she scares me to death the way she drives. . .looks everywhere but at the road. . .I won't ride with her any more")*

—When our car came around bend in road (approx. 500-700 feet from inter.) *I saw traffic light over intersection red for us. . .Calhoon slowed maybe 5-10 m.p.h. . .when we came within 10 to 15 feet of the intersection traffic light changed to green for us. . .we kept going into intersection and was hit by other car. . .*(could have been 2-3 car lengths from inter.)

—Car was a VW driven by **William Morris** (address unknown) with several passengers (names & addresses unknown). . .going north on E. 185th St. . .don't know how fast other car going, *but plenty fast. . .over the speed limit (35 m.p.h.) I'm sure.* (End of Page 1)   *M.C.*

—Saw other car few seconds before crash. . .*hollered to Calhoon "Stop. . .there's a car coming". . .Calhoon kept going.*

—*Our car hit in right side at right front fender. . .*had my seat belt on *but Calhoon didn't (said she never uses it)*

—I wasn't hurt. . .*Calhoon said was dizzy but not hurt. . .Morris came over our car after. . .said he saw our car coming and thought we'd stop. . .he accused Calhoon of running stop light. . .she said she didn't.*

—Calhoon had 2 martinis during lunch. . .I had nothing to drink. . *she told me later she never saw light change from red to green, but thought it was always green.*

—Calhoon said her neck hurt the day after accident. . .*still complains. . .holds her head stiff like. . .I think she's exaggerating. . .she didn't complain about her neck right after accident.*

In writing this summary in longhand, the lawyer distinguished between favorable facts (bold face type) and unfavorable facts (italic type), using underlines, single for the former and double for the latter. Do you know now which party he represented? If you are still uncertain, the statement he wrote from the facts is a giveaway.

Statement of Mary Campana
taken at #615 Union Commerce Bldg.,
Cleveland, O.
January 5, 1971

My name is Mary Campana. I am 52 years of age, married to John Campana and live at 1632 Canterbury Rd., Cleveland, O., with my husband and 2 sons, Harold and Kenneth.

At about 2 p.m., Monday, December 21, 1970, I was involved in a 2 car accident. I was a passenger in a 1968 Plymouth 2 door sedan driven by Mrs. Reba Calhoon, 1628 Canterbury Rd., Cleveland, O. I sat next to her in the front seat.

Reba and I had been to a style show and luncheon at the Statler Hilton Hotel, Euclid Ave., Cleveland, and were driving eastbound on the inside lane of Lake Shore Blvd. Our car was hit by a Volkswagen at the intersection of Lake Shore Blvd. and E. 185th St., Euclid, O. The other driver was a William Morris. I don't know his address. There were 2 passengers in his car whose names and addresses I don't know.

Here's the way the accident happened. It was entirely Mr. Morris' fault.

As our car was going east and approaching the intersection it was moving about 30 miles per hour. The traffic light over the intersection was red for us. Reba slowed to about 20 miles per hour and when we were maybe 3 car lengths from the intersection the traffic light changed to green for eastbound Lake Shore traffic.

Reba started into the intersection after the light turned green. Our car was still moving about 20 miles per hour as we entered the intersection. I saw the VW approaching from our right on E. 185th St. It was going plenty fast. . .faster than 35 miles per hour, I'm sure.

Instead of stopping, the other car kept coming. Our car was already in the intersection when the VW entered it and struck us. It never slowed down before hitting us. The front end of the VW hit the right side of our car, just in front of the passenger door.

After the crash Reba told me she was dizzy. Later she said her neck hurt. She still complains of pain in her neck and holds her head stiff like because her neck hurts.

Right after he hit us, while we were still in our car, Mr. Morris walked over and said that he'd seen our car coming but thought we were going to stop. I don't know why he thought that since we had the green light. I know the traffic light was green for us. I saw it and Reba told me she saw it. It definitely turned green while we were still some distance from the intersection.

I don't know why Mr. Morris didn't stop for his red light. Maybe he was looking at us or at his passengers instead of paying attention to the traffic light.

I have read this 2 page statement and it is true.

Mary Campana

Critique Of The Statement

It must be obvious from a comparison of the statement with the summary of facts that the writer represents claimant Reba Calhoon. Notice the features that make it unusually effective in achieving its purposes:

—It is understandable. The language is simple and conversational.
—It is readable. Sentences and paragraphs are short.
—The narrative is animated. The first person and active voice are used.
—It is properly slanted. Every favorable fact (bold face type in summary) is included and every unfavorable fact (italics in summary) is excluded.
—It projects authenticity by using the witness' expressions. (". . .when we were maybe 3 car lengths. . ."; ". . ." holds her head stiff like". . .)
—It highlights the favorable mode by emphasis ("It was entirely Mr. Morris' fault") and repetition (the green traffic light is mentioned 4 times).

Figure 6-1 is the diagram that accompanied Mrs. Campana's statement. Note that it shows the positions of both cars *"when the light turned green,"* and that it is also signed by Mrs. Campana.

Section C.   STATEMENTIZING THE ADVERSE PARTY AND UNFRIENDLY WITNESS

UNDERSTANDING THE PURPOSES OF THEIR STATEMENT

As valuable as a client or friendly witness statement is, the adverse party or unfriendly witness statement is considerably more so. The difference is between preparing your own guns to fire at the enemy and being able to fire his own guns back at him, in addition to your own.

For all its value, the statement of your own witness is a one-dimensional aid. Pursuing the weapon metaphor, it is no weapon itself, but a holster that houses the weapon of favorable facts. By contrast, the statement of an enemy is three dimensional. It is, foremost, a weapon. . .admissible itself in evidence as an admission against his interest or to accomplish an impeachment. Furthermore, it packs two weapons rather than one; facts that favor you as an advocate, and facts that hurt him as a witness. The first tends to prove your issues and the second tends to discredit him.

ACTION RULE: An adverse party or unfriendly witness statement must contain facts unfavorable to you or he will never sign or otherwise

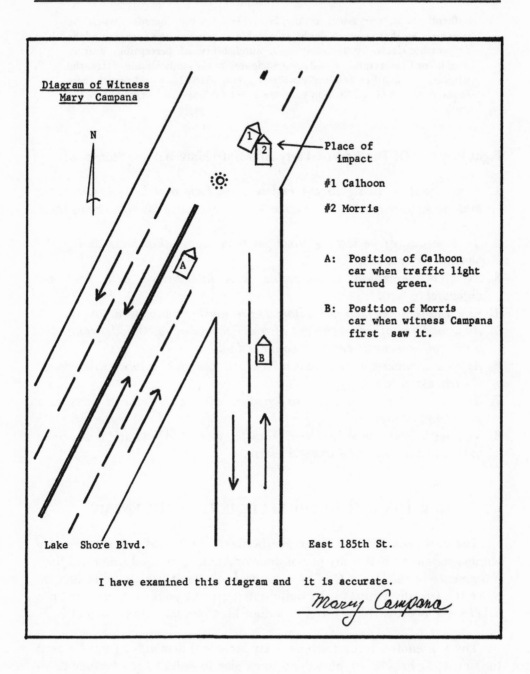

Figure 6-1

authenticate it, nor assent to the favorable facts you include. Design the statement so that as much doubt as possible attaches to the accuracy of the unfavorable facts—by revealing bias, unreliability of perception, hearsay origin, or conjectural quality. Anticipate other unfavorable facts the witness. . .or another unfriendly witness. . .may assert later and negate them in the statement (e.g., "I didn't see the other car until an instant before the crash").

Eight Purposes Of The Adverse Party And Unfriendly Witness Statement

1. *As a record of all significant and relevant facts pertaining to your case that are known to the witness, made at a time when his memory of them is fresh.*
2. *As a means of refreshing your memory about his facts during the pendancy of the case.*
3. *As a memorandum of favorable facts interspersed with necessary unfavorable facts.*
4. *As a lead to other facts and witnesses previously unknown to you.*
5. *As a medium of impeachment at trial because of falsehoods, contradictions and/or inconsistent facts contained within.*
6. *As an evidentiary exhibit at trial when it contains an admission against the witness' interest.*
7. *As a means of preparing your cross-examination of the witness at a deposition or trial.*
8. *As a settlement lever, fashioned from the favorable facts and impeaching material collected and displayed within.*

HOW TO WRITE UP THE STATEMENT OF THE ENEMY

The most conspicuous difference between the friendly and unfriendly witness statement is the absence of unfavorable facts in the former and their prominence in the latter. Odd as it seems, both result from good technique. Since the friendly witness is by definition partial to your case, you need not balance the sweet with the bitter to induce his approval of the statement.

The unfriendly witness (adverse party included) demands a price for even the unwitting help he supplies. You must give in order to get. Include in his statement facts that hurt your case so that he will approve other facts or denials that help. It is a form of strategy that La Rochefoucauld said is common in human affairs:

"We confess little faults in order to establish a larger virtue."

Before commencing to write the statement, review the general techniques of effective statement writing presented earlier in the chapter. Now consider the following techniques designed to achieve the special purposes of this type statement. Use both sets as your writing guide; they will lead you safely and surely to your goal, which is to play the termite with your opponent's case.

Checklist For Producing An Effective Statement

—Write or type up the statement in the witness' home or office immediate-following your interview and in his presence.

—From your interview notes, identify facts that are relevant to some issue of your case or the witness' credibility (e.g., as to credibility, facts showing his position when he claims to have perceived unfavorable facts. . .indicating difficulty, improbability or faultiness of the perception). Since your time with this witness is limited, do not bother to number his fact statements. Sacrifice order in favor of expedition.

—From the facts so identified, distinguish between those that are unfavorable to your case and those that are favorable. In this context, an unfavorable fact tends to prove one or more of the claims or defenses of your opponent. A favorable fact tends to disprove one or more of your opponent's claims or defenses, impairs the witness' credibility, *or negates some unfavorable fact which he or some other unfriendly witness may assert.* (e.g., as to the last. . . "Both my passengers told me later they didn't see the traffic light and don't know whether it was red or green at the time of the accident.")

—Now proceed to write or type the statement, including some of the unfavorable facts *and all the favorable facts*, so it presents the following information in narrative form:

1. Identity and address of the witness; place and date of the statement.
2. Facts establishing a foundation for the witness or showing an inadequate foundation for his expressed perceptions. (i.e., where he was and when, what he did, and when and where he did it)
3. Several unfavorable facts relevant to one or more of the opposing claims or defenses.
4. All favorable facts interspersed as much as possible among the unfavorable facts to avoid a cumulative adverse effect.

    Note: Include the witness' opinion of your client's fault, liability or guilt in emphatic terms. It does you no harm, since it is an opinion and not a fact, but can do much good. His suspicion of you and opposition to inclusion of favorable facts is often quelled by the sight of such heavy condemnation.

Note: Don't be afraid that inclusion of favorable facts will block his approval and authentication of the statement. Even if he insists on striking a statement or two, have him do the striking himself. By doing so. . .and initialing it. . .he authenticates without a signature.

—*Whenever the witness is imprecise* about an unfavorable or favorable fact, speaks in generalities or estimates over a range of values, construe it most liberally in your favor. Write down the most favorable specific or value encompassed by the generality or fitting in the range. (e.g., If the witness says your client was "drunk", write that he "staggered" or "had the smell of alcohol about him" after the accident. If the witness says your client was driving "anywhere from 60 to 80 miles per hour", write that he was driving "about 60 miles per hour.")

—*Do not give the witness a copy of his statement*. Even though in the case of an adverse party statement, his counsel can get a copy (Federal Rule of Civil Procedure #26 and State counterparts) make him use discovery to get it. . .or wait until you show it during settlement negotiations. The sooner he gets a copy, the more time he has to seek to avoid its consequences.

—*Whenever the witness' facts describe a scene* or refer to an event occurring at a scene (e.g., accident or crime scene and the event which occurred there; location and extent of real or personal property damage) make a diagram on a separate page of the statement consistent with his statement facts.

—*Make one or two obvious but essentially insignificant errors* in both the statement and diagram, anticipating that the witness may refuse to sign or otherwise authenticate them. (See the statement example that follows.) Have him correct the errors in his own hand. Even the most recalcitrant witness will usually do so.

—*Give the statement and diagram to the witness to read*. Ask him to correct any mistake, then sign both, after writing the appropriate following sentences in his own hand:

I have read this (#) page statement and it is true.
I have examined this diagram and it is accurate.

In addition, have him sign or initial the bottom of each page of a multi-page statement. Whenever a correction is made by you or him, have him initial it.

Note: Many unfriendly witnesses will refuse to sign or initial anything for you, fearing a trick or injury they cannot name. But most of these will consent to write the postscript sentence, never realizing that their handwriting is as much an authentication as the other. Even if they refuse this, their correction of mistakes is enough.

EXAMPLE OF AN UNFRIENDLY WITNESS INTERVIEW FACTS AND STATEMENT

Here is a listing of facts obtained from the adverse party, William Morris, in the case in which Reba Calhoon was claimant. Her attorney interviewed Morris at the latter's home, marshalled his facts and then wrote the statement that follows. Note that before commencing the statement he distinguished unfavorable from favorable facts, using single underlines (shown as Italics) for the first and double lines (shown as boldface type) for the second. By doing so, he knew in advance which facts he would use and which he would omit. The lawyer's selection of facts for inclusion and his phrasing of the facts used were not challenged by Morris.

As you read the list of facts, assume for a moment that you are counsel for claimant. How will you write the statement? What facts will you include and how will you recite them? Then examine the Morris statement and decide whether your product or this one is the stronger.

Before savoring the triumph. . .should the vote go to you. . .remember you don't have an adverse party sitting across from you demanding that your handiwork satisfy him.

Summary Of Facts Obtained During Interview With William Morris

—41 years old, married to Julie. . .lives at 18501 Kildeer Ave., Euclid, with wife, 4 daughters, Robin, Carol, Dawn and Debbie. . .all minors.
—Driving 1965 VW 2 door sedan. . .he owns. . .with 2 passengers, Fred Miller, 18903 Muskoka Ave., Euclid and Tom Jurjanz, 19700 Miller Ave., Euclid.
—Involved in 2 car accident with '68 Plymouth driven by Reba Calhoon. . .1 female passenger in Calhoon car. . .name and address unknown. . .accident happened about 2:30 p.m., Monday, December 21, 1970. . .intersection of Lake Shore Blvd. and E. 185th St., Euclid.
—Going north on E. 185th about 30-35 m.p.h. . .approaching intersection. . . *traffic light above center of inter. green*. . .assumes light red for eastbound Lake Shore traffic *but couldn't see.*

—*Slowed to 20 m.p.h. as started into intersection. . .saw Calhoon on left but assumed she'd stop. . .don't know what speed Calhoon car. . .looked fast to him.*

—*Drove into inter. turning to go east on Lake Shore Blvd. when Calhoon car struck by left front corner. . .right front corner of C car damaged.*

—I talked to Calhoon after. . .asked if she was hurt. . *she said she felt bad but not hurt. . .I don't remember anything else said between us. . .*no talk with C passenger.

—*Collision severe. . .I was shaken up but not hurt. . .*saw no doctor. . .missed no time from work. . .*my passengers not hurt either. . .they told me ok. . .*saw them since at work and no complaints of pain.

—*Positive light green for me when entered intersection. . .about 5-7 car lenghts from light when remember looking at it. . .green then. . .don't remember looking at it again* but sure it was still green.

—*Both my passengers told me don't know what happened. . .talking to each other before crash and not paying attention outside car.*

—*My car damaged front bumper, left front fender, left headlight, left side grill. . .*repaired Swanson's Garage, E. 140th St. . .$385.00. . .repair bill less $100 paid by my insurer. . .Allstate Ins. Co. . .has *100,000/300,000/ 10,000 liability coverages.*

—*Calhoon car damaged right front fender, front of passenger door.*

—Euclid police investigated. . .questioned drivers separately. . .told them same facts as here. . .no arrests. . *.police said no skid marks his car.*

—Interview on January 10, 1971 at witness residence. . .about 9 p.m.

Statement of William Morris
taken at 18501 Kildeer Ave., Euclid, O.
January 10, 1971

My name is William Morris and I live at the above address with my wife and four daughters. On Monday, December 21, 1970, at about 2:30 p.m., I was involved in a two car accident at the intersection of E. 185th St. and Lake Shore Blvd. in Euclid. I was driving a 1965 VW in a northerly direction on E. 185th St.

I drove into the intersection and was turning to go east on Lake Shore when my car was hit by a 1968 Plymouth being driven by a Reba Calhoon. She was driving east on Lake Shore at the time.

There were 2 passengers in my car, Fred Miller, 18903 Muskoka Ave., Euclid, and Tom Jurjanz, 19700 Miller Ave., Euclid. I understand from talking to both of them afterward that neither one *say how the accident happened. They said they were talking to each other at the time and paying no attention outside the car.*

In my opinion Mrs. Calhoon was at fault for this accident. There is a traffic light above the intersection and it was green for me and red for her. I actually could not see the color of the light facing her but I assume it was red because it was green for me.

I was going about 35 m.p.h. just before I got to the intersection and slowed somewhat when I started into it. I was about seven car lengths away from the intersection when I looked at the light and saw it was green for me. I don't remember looking at the light again but I'm sure it stayed green. (page 1)

I saw the Calhoon car coming from my right when I came near the intersection but I assumed she would stop and so I continued into it. I don't know how fast her car was going.

I don't know whether Mrs. Calhoon was hurt or not but I don't think she was. I asked her if she was hurt and she said she felt bad. I don't remember anything else that was said between us.

It was a hard collision all right. My car was damaged in the front bumper, left front fender, left headlight and left side grill. It was repaired by Swanson's Garage, E. 140th St., Cleveland, for $385.00. My insurance company, Allstate Insurance, paid all but $100.00 of the bill. I have a liability policy with this company with $100,000/300,000/10,000 coverage.

The Calhoon car was damaged in the right front fender and the front of the passenger side door.

I was shaken up in the accident but not injured. I didn't see a doctor and haven't missed any time from work. Neither one of my passengers was hurt. At least they told me they wasn't hurting anywhere.

The Euclid police investigated and talked to us separately. I don't know what Mrs. Calhoon told them. I told them what I'm saying here. The police officer told me that my car left no skid marks. I didn't check myself.

Critique Of The Morris Statement

Compare the statement with the summary of interview facts and see how adroitly the lawyer handled his material. He has a statement that is pure gold, minimizing the unfavorable, maximizing the favorable and replete with impeachment potential. Moreover, it is so demonstrably genuine, even without a signature, that only a desperate or foolhardy defense counsel would challenge it. Consider these strengths:

—*Unfavorable facts are eliminated* (e.g., "slowed to 20 m/p/h" in the interview summary becomes "slowed somewhat" in the statement. . ."she said she felt bad but wasn't hurt" becomes "she said she felt bad").

—*Unfavorable generalities are minimized* (e.g., "going. . .about 30-35 m/p/h" becomes "going about 35 m/p/h". . ."about 5-7 car lengths from the intersection when (he saw the green light)" becomes "about 7 car lengths. . .")

—*Negative facts are stated which preclude later assertions by Morris or his passengers* (e.g., "(the passengers said they were) paying no attention outside the car". . ."I don't remember looking at the light again (after his car was 7 car lengths from the intersection)". . ."I was shaken up in the accident but not injured". . .(the passengers) "told me they wasn't hurting anywhere")

—*Impeachment is accomplished from inconsistent facts* (Morris claims the Calhoon car hit him, but the location of damage to the cars, as he describes it, clearly shows his car hit hers)

—*Liability insurance coverage is discovered and stated.* This evidences to defense counsel that claimant's counsel knows the high coverage limits—a factor that enhances the likelihood and size of settlement before suit.

—*The statement is adequately authenticated.* Although Morris refused to sign at the end, he corrected the deliberate mistake ("I saw the Calhoon car coming from my right. . .") initialed page 1 and wrote the attestation in his own hand.

Epilogue To The Case Of Calhoon v Morris

The lawyer for Mrs. Calhoon was unable to get a diagram from Mr. Morris. As it developed, the diagram was not needed. The case was settled for $3,500 soon after suit was filed, largely on the strength of the Campana and Morris statements. Since the injury was a cervical strain (whiplash) and out-of-pocket expenses totalled $425, the settlement must be accounted a plantiff's victory.

Section D: STATEMENTIZING THE DISINTERESTED WITNESS

Earlier in this guide, interviewing techniques were presented to interest disinterested witnesses in your client's welfare—to induce a favorable bias in one who, by definition, is unbiased. This section presents techniques for carrying that bias into a paper monument, the written witness statement, to promote a "good" settlement and insure "good" testimony if no settlement comes.

Why This Witness Scores So Well. . .Sometimes Mistakenly

If artfully constructed, the disinterested witness statement will carry the greatest negotiating clout with your opponent, even as his testimony carries the greatest evidentiary clout with a judge and jury. This is so because, having no stake in the outcome of the case, it is supposed he must be perfectly impartial.

But experience shows us otherwise. There is a very human tendency to choose sides even without the promise of gain. Who can watch any sports contest on television without picking a favorite? It may stem from a variety of reasons—sympathy for weakness, some distant association or other, or even the color of one team's uniform.

Whatever the cause, the same tendency exists in disinterested witnesses. Exploit it! To the end that a neutral is converted into a friend. . .a friend who will, in a close case, emphasize favorable facts and subordinate unfavorable ones on his own and allow you to do so in his statement.

> **ACTION RULE: Induce a favorable bias in the disinterested witness using techniques presented in Chapter 3. Then, design his statement to take advantage of the bias by including all favorable facts and as few unfavorable facts as he will tolerate. But. . .**
>
> **If he is hostile or his facts are dominantly unfavorable, lay the basis for his impeachment. Include in his statement denials of other unfavorable facts to preclude a later assertion of them. Also include inconsistencies and contradictions in his facts wherever they exist.**

Since he is neither controlled by you nor by your opponent, you cannot know with certainty when you statementize him in which camp he will eventually pitch his tent. . .for which party he will testify if your case must be tried and who will benefit most from that testimony.

The purposes of a disinterested witness statement reflect this uncertainty whether he will be a friend or enemy. You must prepare for the first and provide for the second.

SIX PURPOSES OF THE DISINTERESTED WITNESS STATEMENT

1. *As a memorandum of all favorable facts emphasized to the degree that is acceptable to the witness and containing as few unfavorable facts as he will countenance.*
2. *As a means of refreshing your memory of his facts during the pendancy of the case.*
3. *As a means of refreshing the witness' memory of his facts, according to your selection and emphasis, during the pendancy of the case. . .to prepare him to answer your opponent's questions at an interview or deposition.*
4. *As a means of preparing the witness to testify at trial.*
5. *As a settlement lever embodying a strength in your case. . .favorable facts told by one who is prepared to repeat them in court and unfavorable facts diluted and minimized.*
6. *As a medium of impeachment at trial, if necessary, because of negations, contradictions and/or inconsistent facts contained within.*

HOW TO WRITE UP THE
STATEMENT OF THE PROFESSED NEUTRAL

Techniques for achieving these purposes practice a species of brinksmanship. The witness is neither as tractable as a friendly witness nor as resistant as an unfriendly one. Properly oriented toward a sympathetic outlook, he will usually go along with a weighted statement up to a limit, with the limit exceeded when he is asked to certify a known untruth, an obvious exaggeration or facts exclusively favoring your client.

Your statement-writing objective, then, must be to find the witness' limit and crowd it constantly without breaking through and antagonizing him.

Before commencing to write his statement, review the general techniques of effective statement writing presented earlier in the chapter. Now consider the following further techniques for achieving the purposes of this type statement.

CHECKLIST OF WHAT TO DO FOR
A PRODUCTIVE AND PROTECTIVE STATEMENT

—*Write or type up the statement in the witness' home or office. . .*or your office if you managed to interview him there. . .and in his presence.

—*From your completed witness checklist form* and other interview notes, identify facts that are relevant to some issue of your case.

—*From the facts so identified,* distinguish between favorable and unfavorable.

—*Now proceed to write or type the statement, including all the favorable facts and only such unfavorable facts as are innocuous,* i.e. they neither alone nor collectively disprove any one of your claims or defenses (you can state that your client was driving "quite fast," but never state that he was going "about 70 m.p.h. in a 60 m.p.h. zone"),

—*Also include in the statement negations* of significant unfavorable facts to preclude his later asserting them (e.g., your client's car was going "quite fast, but I didn't see it long enough to form an opinion as to its speed.")

—*If the witness appears hostile* or his facts are predominantly unfavorable, include facts in the statement that impair his credibility (e.g., facts showing his position when he claims to have perceived unfavorable facts. . .indicating difficulty, improbability, or faultiness of the perception). Also include any and all inconsistencies and/or contradictions that appear in his unfavorable facts (e.g., he says that your client did not appear to stop for the stop sign, then says he didn't see the client's car until it was in the intersection. . .omit the first statement and include the second.)

—*Whenever the witness is imprecise about a favorable fact,* speaks in generalities or estimates over a range of values, construe it most liberally in your favor. Write down the most favorable specific or value encompassed by the generality or fitting in the range. (e.g., if he says the adverse party "appeared to be intoxicated after the accident," write that he was "drunk." If he says the party was driving "anywhere from 60 to 80 m.p.h.," write that he was driving "about 80 m.p.h.")

Note: Don't be afraid to test the witness' limits as to favorable constructions in this way. If he balks you can change it. But if he assents to it, this is the way he will testify to it later.

—*Give the witness a copy of his statement.* Ask him to keep it in a safe place and to read it over from time to time to refresh his recollections. Warn him that your opponent will probably interview him. *Don't suggest that he refuse to talk with the lawyer.* But *do* suggest that he read over your statement carefully before this interview so his answers are consistent with facts he has attested there.

—*Whenever the witness' facts describe a scene* or refer to an event occurring at a scene (e.g., accident or crime scene and the event which occurred there; location and extent of real or personal property damage) make a diagram on a separate page of the statement consistent with his statement facts.

—*Give the statement and diagram to the witness to read.* Ask him to correct any mistake, then sign both, after writing the appropriate following sentences of attestation at the end:

"I have read this (#) page statement and it is true."
"I have examined this diagram and it is accurate."

In addition, have him sign or initial the bottom of each page of a multi-page statement. Whenever a correction is made by you or him, have him initial it.

7

Productive Settlement Techniques
For Civil Damage Cases

TABLE OF CONTENTS

Productive Settlement Techniques
For Civil Damage Cases

*"Every lawyer should be a specialist in negotiation. His first
concern should be the prevention of litigation."*

INTRODUCTION TO PART III:
WINNING SETTLEMENT TECHNIQUES

Today, some fifty years after Dean Pound delivered the message, the
necessity for effective negotiation is even more acute. Pound pressed the
public interest when he spoke, but client interest is also served by
settlement.

Litigation is so expensive and victory from it so uncertain in most cases
that it should be the last resort rather than the first. From the client's
standpoint, the first and foremost reason is the added expense of
litigation—the increase in his attorney's fees. If his contract is on an hourly
basis, litigation prolongs the running of the clock. Even the contingent fee
contract will likely be affected, since it commonly provides for an increased
percentage fee once suit is filed.

And extra attorney fees from litigation is only a beginning. Expert
witnesses must be hired and fee'd. Then there is discovery, court reporters to
pay, transcripts to finance.

If only a favorable outcome of suit was certain, what client would be
injured and what lawyer deterred by extra expense? But it never is.
Paraphrasing Wilde, few lawyers ever expect what they get and fewer clients
ever get what they expect. Jurors are influenced by factors other than
evidence (exemplified by the cartoon showing one juror saying to another,
"I try to keep an open mind and not let the evidence influence me"). And
judges are influenced by factors other than law.

Why Early Settlement Benefits Counsel As Well As Client

Since time is the lawyer's raw material, it limits your income to the available supply and it should be obvious why early case settlements, so long as they are favorable—or at least fair—benefit you.

Hourly-fee'd lawyers who close two cases for the price of one in another lawyers' hands quickly gain a reputation for efficiency. Soon clients and cases meant for the others begin gravitating their way until at last they achieve the pinnacle of any lawyer's desire. *They can select from among their cases those they wish to work on, for interest or for profit, assigning the remainder to associates.*

Contingent-fee'd lawyers do even better. No cast of the dice for them. For every settlement there is a fee, and even though it may be less than if the case was sued to a favorable judgment, less was done to earn it. . .less time, less work, less risk.

Why Negotiating Technique Is Vital To Good Settlemeents

Although the need and advantage of early settlement has increased mightily since Dean Pound's day, the number of negotiating specialists has not. Negotiating and dispute settlement techniques are disdained in law schools, devalued in Bar circles, and discounted by many lawyers.

> 'There's nothing to negotiating a settlement," one lawyer told me. "If you've got a good case, they'll offer a lot. And if you've got a bad case, you'll take anything."

I saw this lawyer demonstrate his approach to negotiating at many a pre-trial conference and it seems that he believes there is nothing to it because he gets nothing from it. He does everything wrong. He never evaluates his evidence, witnesses, law and opposing counsel to find a fair settlement value. When he represents plaintiff he makes a demand, always excessive, which he thinks a jury may award him under ideal conditions. Then he never budges more than slightly from this position.

When he represents defendant he is arbitrary the other way.

Besides these flaws of policy, there are flaws of behavior. He is arrogant and opinionated, disputing every statement his opponent makes even though it is clear he doesn't know the facts. He enters negotiations with only the foggiest notion of case facts and law. Clearly, he never bothers to review his statements or research the law beforehand.

There is no stage of a case more vital to defeat or victory than the moment of serious settlement negotiation before suit is filed or an indictment returned. Like negotiations between hostile nations the outcome determines whether there shall be peace or war. . .peace with fair objectives achieved or war with ruin risked.

With such consequences in the balance, negotiations in civil and criminal cases cannot be entered with indifference and ineptitude, as though it was a routine stop along the road to trial. *You must prepare for negotiation as thoroughly as you prepare for trial and bring as many good techniques to the negotiating table as you bring to the trial table.*

The Test Of A Good Settlement

The surest test of a good settlement is its relationship to the probable outcome of trial. Will a trial of your civil case probably result in a defense verdict, will your criminal defendant be convicted on the indictment? Then a settlement resulting in more than nothing in the first case or less than everything in the second is a good settlement.

But how does one determine the probable outcome of a trial? And how does he use this determination to bargain for something better? This is where technique enters the picture, for it is by knowing and using good settlement techniques that these questions are answered.

> **ACTION RULE: Civil Cases: Approach each negotiating session with the belief that your case can and will be settled favorably. This conviction will insure that you do the work of preparation that you must. It will also communicate itself to opposing counsel at the session itself and often breed a responsive conviction to him, transforming a one-sided exercise into a bilateral accomplishment.**
>
> **Determine the fair settlement value of your case by knowing and applying the factors that affect it. Then, know how to bargain to achieve or better the settlement value and utilize those techniques.**
>
> **ACTION RULE: Criminal Cases: Approach each negotiating session with the conviction that a dismissal or favorable plea can be induced, in order to realize the same psychological and result benefits as in civil cases.**

> Determine the probable trial outcome of your case by knowing and applying the factors that will affect it. Then, know how to bring bargaining and other pressures to bear on the prosecutor to better that outcome by inducing a dismissal or consent to a lesser plea. . .and utilize these techniques.

Chapters 7-9 present techniques for repeatedly achieving good settlements in civil and criminal cases, consistent with the rules just stated. Chapters 7 and 8 concern civil cases; 7 discusses techniques of general efficacy for both plaintiff and defense counsel, and 8 presents special techniques of value each counsel separately. Chapter 9 is devoted to settlement techniques profiting defense counsel in criminal cases.

In whatever role your case casts you, whether representing plaintiff or defendant, you cannot make a serious demand or offer of settlement without basing it on some notion of your case value. Only a foolish or frivolous lawyer does otherwise.

How does this notion of value arise? Consciously or unconsciously, it comes from a prediction you make as to the verdict a jury or judge will return if the case is tried. To the extent that your prediction is accurate, taking into account all known factors influencing trial outcome, to just such an extent will your opinion of case value be accurate. And if your opinion of value is accurate, then your settlement objective that is based upon it represents a good result.

But trial outcome is only one of several factors that determines settlement value. All should be weighed before negotiations commence.

> ACTION RULE: Before making a serious settlement offer or demand, determine the fair settlement value of your case by applying and evaluating the seven factors that affect it.

SEVEN FACTORS AFFECTING SETTLEMENT VALUE

1. *The probability that the verdict after trail will be either for plaintiff or defendant.* This factor depends upon thorough knowledge of the available evidence and applicable law relating to each liability issue of your case. Therefore, before this probability can be determined and measured, your fact investigation and preliminary research must be completed to the fullest extent possible before suit or indictment.

2. *The probable verdict range if it is for the plaintiff.* There are three components underlying an accurate estimate of verdict range; 1) a thorough knowledge of all available evidence (yours and opponent's) relating to damage or remedy issues; 2) an understanding of principles of law applied in your jurisdiction to prescribe the "measure of damages" or extent of equitable relief; 3) a knowledge of past verdicts returned recently in your jurisdiction in reasonably similar cases (your jurisdiction's jury "posture" on damages as evidenced by actual verdicts in analogous cases).

3. *The collectibility of any judgment that plaintiff obtains.* Obtaining a judgment carries a plaintiff only part way to his goal. He must convert it to cash before he is satisfied. There are literally thousands of impressive judgments recorded in every state which, like pre-World War II Deutschemarks, are not worth the paper they are written on—because the defendant cannot pay them.

   The fair settlement value of your case, then, is affected by the ease, difficulty, or impossibility of collecting whatever judgment plaintiff wins. To determine collectibility, you must investigate the nature and extent of assets available to pay the judgment (e.g., liability insurance policy and dollar limits thereunder; the net worth of the corporate or individual defendant).

4. *The probable cost of obtaining a plaintiff's judgment.* You should estimate the reasonable expenses plaintiff will incur beginning with the filing of suit through trial (e.g., extra attorney fees, expert witness fees, discovery expenses). Clearly, fair settlement value should reflect the savings plaintiff will realize from settlement.

5. *The probable cost of collecting a plaintiff's judgment.* Estimate the reasonable expenses plaintiff will probably incur from the time he obtains judgment until he collects all he can on it. This item should include additional attorney fees and expenses incident to a defense appeal of the judgment (many contingent fee contracts provide an additional percentage to the lawyer for resisting an appeal—and many insurance company and corporate defendants routinely appeal every judgment not to their liking). Also include estimated expenses in locating and levying upon assets of an individual defendant.

   Again, fair settlement value should reflect the savings plaintiff will realize from settlement.

6. *The probable cost of the defense.* Estimate the reasonable expenses defendant will incur, beginning with the response to the complaint through trial to a final conclusion. Include the substantial additional

attorney fees defending the suit and also fees for prosecuting or defending an appeal, depending on trial outcome. Add to this total estimate a reasonable sum for pre-trial and trial expenses, including expert witness and investigator fees and discovery costs.

7. *The capability of yourself and opposing counsel.* Not many lawyers can achieve a silk purse result from a sow's ear case. Few miracles occur in the courtroom. But, a skilled trial lawyer is able to do consistently better with the cases he has than an incompetent. Since lawyer capability is a factor affecting trial outcome, it should also be a factor influencing fair settlement value. It is a factor in the consideration of every liability insurance carrier, those specialists in settlement negotiation, who shape their offers not only to the merit of claimants' cases but to the merit of their lawyers as well.

Evaluate your pre-trial and trial strength and that of your opponent as objectively as possible, having in mind such considerations as experience, reputation within the local Bar, and past litigation results.

The first two of these seven factors, the probable winner, and the verdict range if the winner is plaintiff, are the most difficult to determine and the most crucial to an accurate fair settlement value. Here are techniques for determining them.

CHECKLIST FOR PREDICTING
THE PROBABLE VERDICT WINNER

—*Complete your investigation of facts* by securing all relevant documents available to you, identifying, interviewing and statementizing the important witnesses and visiting the scene of your case event.

—*If you represent claimant,* determine the precise cause(s) of action your client has under the facts gathered. Further determine from the facts and statements whether an affirmative defense (defenses) is indicated or claimed.

—*If you represent defendant,* determine the cause(s) of action suggested by the facts or asserted by claimant. Further, determine from the facts whether an affirmative defense (defenses) is indicated.

—*If there is counsel representing defendant,* then whatever side you are on, discuss the case with your opponent to learn the cause(s) or defense(s) he asserts and his factual basis for either.

—*Determine the precise legal issues claimant must prove to recover a judgment upon his cause(s)* (If his cause is based on a negligent injury, the issues are: 1) that defendant was negligent; and 2) that his negligence proximately caused plaintiff's injury).

—*Determine the precise legal issue(s) defendant must prove to recover a judgment upon an asserted affirmative defense* that plaintiff was also negligent; and 2) that his negligence proximately caused or contributed to cause his injury).

> *Note: If you are doubt about either set of issues, research the legal theory of recovery (e.g., negligence, assault and battery, breach of contract, nuisance) or defense (e.g., contributory negligence, estoppel, privilege) to ascertain the necessary elements of proof. If your jurisdiction has adopted official jury instructions you can usually find the issues specified under the appropriate theory of recover. Consult American Jurisprudence and your own state legal encyclopedia under the proper theory heading for a more wordy but accurate statement of issues.*

—*Make a list of the liability issues* applicable to your case. Now review your facts, documents and statements and determine what witnesses and evidence will likely be available to you and your opponent at the time of trial pertaining to each issue. For easier evaluating, summarize the evidence and write it down under the proper issue heading.

—*Determine by what degree of proof plaintiff must prove his issues* for recovery and defendant must prove his issues of affirmative defense. (Generally, all issues of recovery or affirmative defense must be proved by a preponderance of evidence.)

—*Now determine from the summary of available evidence whether either side is entitled to a judgment as a matter of law.* If plaintiff has no available evidence on some issue essential to his recovery, defendant is entitled to judgment as of law. If plaintiff's evidence is so strong on *all* his essential issues that "reasonable minds" must agree that he has succeeded in proving them by the proper degree of evidence, then judgment as a matter of law must be given plaintiff.

Finally, if defendant's evidence on his affirmative defense is so strong that reasonable minds must agree that he has proved the defense by the preponderance of evidence, then judgment must be given him as a matter of law.

Note: In making the determination under this item, place yourself in the position of the trial judge, who must decide whether judgment as a matter of law is proper. Try to examine the evidence and apply the rules just stated as he would. Objectivity is difficult; it is possible if only you make the mental effort to leave the trial table and "mount the bench."

—*If no judgment as a matter of law seems likely for either side*, examine your checklists of witness profiles and evaluate the witnesses who will testify for you and the opponent. Ask yourself what credibility each witness will project to judge and jury; what weight the latter will probably assign to each one's testimony. Now, again assume the objectivity of judge and jury and weigh the available evidence (yours and opponent's) on each issue. If you can fairly say that, *as to every liability issue*, plaintiff's evidence is more probably and persuasive than defendant's evidence, then plaintiff will probably win the judgment.

If, on the other hand, defendant's evidence *on any liability issue* is more probable and persuasive than plaintiff's evidence on the same issue, then defendant will probably win the judgment.

CHECKLIST FOR DETERMINING THE PROBABLE SIZE OF THE VERDICT

Now that you have determined which party will probably win the verdict if your case is tried, continue with your calculation of the fair settlement value. Measure the size of the verdict if plaintiff wins. Here are techniques for determining it.

—*First, determine the precise "measure of damages" that applies to plaintiff's cause(s) of action.* For example, if the cause is a negligent personal injury, the measure is compensation for all expenses, injury, disability, and pain and suffering proximately caused and to be caused by defendant's negligence.

If the cause is a trespass or nuisance injuring real estate permanently, the measure is the difference in market values before and after defendant's acts, plus a sum representing plaintiff's loss of enjoyment of the property.

If the cause lies in breach of contract, the customary measure is compensation for all consequential damages proximately flowing from the breach that were in the reasonable contemplation of the parties, including expenses and loss of profits.

When in doubt about the precise measure of damages your jurisdiction applies, research it! Guesswork promises error and a mistake on this important feature of your case law makes a poor settlement or a trial defeat virtually certain. If your jurisdiction has adopted official jury instructions, you can usually find the measure of damages set out under the appropriate cause category. Also consult your state legal encyclopedia under the same heading.

—*From your summary of case facts,* documents and statements, determine what witnesses and evidence will likely be available to you and your opponent at the time of trial on the issue of damages. For easier evaluating, summarize the evidence for each side and write it down separately.

—*Make a list of plaintiff's liquidated damage claims* that are either undisputed or supported by very persuasive evidence and will probably be accepted by a jury. Strike from the list any claim which is not sanctioned by the measure of damages. Liquidated damages are items having a fixed and certain dollar value that is identified by evidence (e.g., hospital and medical expense, loss of wages, market value of property or the cost of its repair). Such items are often either undisputed or indisputable.

—*Now add this list of liquidated damage items and draw a total sum. This represents the probable floor of a verdict for plaintiff, the minimum dollar recovery.*

—*Make a second list* of plaintiff's unliquidated damage claims, sanctioned by the proper measure of damages, supported by persuasive evidence and which a jury *may* accept as true. Unliquidated damages are items which are amenable to dollar assessment but are not identifiable as a fixed and certain sum by evidence (e.g., a specific bodily injury, physical disability, loss of use or enjoyment, loss of services and pain and suffering). The dollar value for each such item must be determined by the jury.

—*Investigate past plaintiffs' verdicts in your jurisdiction,* based on reasonably similar damage claims, over the last five years. Consult other lawyers in your area, local trial judges and court personnel and your own case records for examples. Also refer to verdict reporting publications in your area law libraries for recent verdicts in cases similar to yours (e.g., Jury Verdict Research, Inc., a Cleveland, Ohio, based company, publishes summaries of verdicts together with their underlying claims and evidence on a regular basis, regionally reported).

—*List all verdicts you discovered* by the above means and find the largest one. Compare it again with your case claims and evidence. If there is a significant difference that enhanced the amount, throw it out and choose the next highest verdict (e.g., if the verdict example was based upon a permanent injury and your case involves none, the verdict is too distorted to be of use).

*The largest acceptable verdict on the list represents the probable
verdict ceiling in your case, the maximum dollar recovery.* While inflation
has steadily increased over the past decade, so has the conservatism of
jurors, according to plaintiff's counsel specialists.

—The two sums you have found, the minimum and maximum dollar
recovery, represent the *probable range of plaintiff's verdict in your case.*

—As the last step, average out these two sums by adding them and dividing
by two. *The quotient represents the probable average plaintiff's verdict.*

A FORMULA FOR FINDING THE FAIR SETTLEMENT VALUE

Even in a scientific area such as chemistry or meteorology, predicting the
nature of a future event affected by changeable factors is a risky business.
The weather forecaster, whose credibility matches that of soothsayers and
tea leaf readers, still renders an important service despite his potential for
error.

Predicting the outcome of a future jury trial is much riskier, yet it, too,
performs a valuable service. *There is no other way half so reliable to
determine a favorable settlement level before the trial.* How can you possibly
tell whether a proposed settlement is "good" unless you look ahead to the
future trial and judge whether its outcome is likely to be "better" or
"worse"?

All trial lawyers I know *do* look ahead; only a few do it intently and
analytically, employing techniques contained in the prior checklists. Other
lawyers look only briefly assessing the future of their cases perfunctorily and
plucking settlement values according to impulse and self-service rather than
according to studied probabilities.

Your aim must be to eliminate the impulsive, unanalytic judgment of
settlement value that leads lawyers to take too little, pay too much, or reject
a decent settlement when they will lose the trial. Finding the fair settlement
value of your case by means provided here is no guarantee that none of the
three calamities will ever happen to you. But it does guarantee that none will
happen as frequently as before.

Once you have determined the probable winner of a verdict in your case
and the probable average verdict amount, if it is for plaintiff, you are ready
to find the fair settlement value—that sum of money that represents a
satisfactory settlement for both parties. There is a simple formula useful in

finding this value on the basis of your predictions and other factors previously discussed.

The Formula

> ACTION RULE: Fair settlement value (FSV) equals the probable average verdict (PAV) multiplied by the percentage probability of a plaintiff's verdict (PPV) minus any uncollectible portion of the product (UV) minus plaintiff's estimated cost in obtaining and collecting the verdict (PC) plus defendant's estimated cost of defense (DC) plus or minus the net value of intangibles (I).

$$PAV \times \%PPV - UV - PC + DC \pm I = FSV$$

Checklist For Substituting Dollars Into The Equation

—*PAV (probable average verdict)* has been determined. (See page 710).

—*%PPV (percentage probability of a plaintiff's verdict)* is a conversion to an estimated percentage of the determination you previously made (see page 708).

If a direct verdict for plaintiff on liability issues is certain, then the percentage you would use in the equation is 90-100%, depending on how certain you are. If the directed verdict seems probable but not certain, the percentage is 80-90%.

If no direct verdict is likely but a jury verdict for plaintiff is *clearly* probable, the percentage would be 60-80%, depending on the relative strength of the two parties' liability cases. If a jury verdict is only *barely* probable, then 51-60% would be the figure you would insert in the question.

When you have predicted a defendant's verdict by applying the checklist items, then the percentage probability of a plaintiff's verdict is, of necessity, under 50. If a directed verdict for defendant is certain, use 0-10%, but if it is only probable, use 10-20%.

If you have predicted a strong probability of a jury verdict for defendant, the percentage figure would be between 20-40%. If, however, a jury verdict for him is only barely probable, the figure you should use is 40-49%.

—*UV (uncollectible portion of a plaintiff's verdict)* is based upon your knowledge of defendant's financial responsibility, the existence or non-existence of an insurance policy or surety bond covering the judgment and the policy or bond dollar limits. (See Section A Chapter 8 for techniques to determine a defendant's financial responsibility and insurance coverage).

Any portion of the product from multiplying PAV by %PPV which you determine to be uncollectible must be subtracted from the product.

—PC *(plaintiff's cost of obtaining and collecting his verdict)* is an estimation of probable pre-trial and trial expenses based upon standard fees and charges in your jurisdiction and the cost items typical to your case. Use your own trial costs experience. A few phone calls to experienced lawyers in your area will quickly give you an idea of the likely costs from their own charges in similar cases.

—DC *(cost of defense)* is an estimation of total costs defendant or his insurer must bear subsequent to suit filing. It includes attorney fees over this period, calculated on the standard hourly fee for your area multiplied by an estimate of total pre-trial hours; also the standard per diem trial fee multiplied by an estimate of trial days your case will take (2-3 days is usual for a case of average complexity tried to a jury).

This cost item also includes discovery and expert witness expenses similar to that which plaintiff must bear.

In making estimates to figure the total defense costs, use your own cost experiences in past civil cases you defended. Again, several phone calls to experienced defense counsel for guidance will result in enough expense data for a reasonably accurate total estimate.

—I *(intangibles)* is a catch-all item that includes six case circumstances having a direct influence on the outcome of trial and, therefore, on fair settlement value. *Add or subtract 5 percent from the net total cash value in your equation for each circumstance that is present in your case, depending on whether it helps or hurts plaintiff.*

1. *Significant counsel advantage.* If either you or your opponent enjoys a decided advantage of skill and experience over the other, add or subtract 5 percent of the settlement value sub-total. This assumes an average pre-trial and trial competence in the other lawyer. If your opponent is a known incompetent add or subtract 10 percent. These percentages conform to the consensus among trial lawyers generally as to the impact of a skill advantage on trial outcome.

2. *There is a "target" defendant.* If the defendant in your case is a large corporation with a high public visibility (e.g., General Motors Corp.) or a smaller company with poor public image (e.g., cab companies, truck lines, junk dealers, auto graveyard operators) add 5 percent from the settlement value sub-total. There is an acknowledged tendency among juries to punish such defendants, either because of dislike or because their affluence makes a payment to plaintiff painless.

3. *Pressing need of plaintiff.* It sometimes happens that plaintiff is in serious financial trouble or has a special need of money as soon as

possible. In such instances, a sum now serves him better than a somewhat larger sum later. The need is usually known to both attorneys or deducible from his circumstances, so both should introduce this circumstance into their equations when it exists. Deduct 5 percent from the settlement value sub-total.

4. *Defendant has a large financial exposure.* An affluent defendant suffers an intangible detriment quite apart from the fact that he or it may also be a "target" defendant. The hazard of the latter is the punitive treatment it will likely receive from the jury. The detriment from affluence exists in the fact that no matter how large plaintiff's verdict may be—within reason—it is collectible. Thus, such defendants have an added incentive to settle their cases. Increase the settlement value sub-total by 5 percent.

5. *The effect of plaintiff's personal profile.* Jurors are influenced not alone by a party's testimony, but also by the party himself. Witness the cartoon in *Case & Comment* some months back. A female juror is explaining her verdict for plaintiff: "I decided the case strictly on the evidence," she says. "The evidence that plaintiff is kind, honest and handsome, while defendant's a mean, spiteful frump."

   Add 5 percent to the settlement value sub-total if the plaintiff will project a strongly sympathetic image (plaintiff is a child or widow; or he or she is clean-cut, well-groomed, and pleasant). Deduct 5 percent if plaintiff projects a strongly negative image (resembles a stereotype "hippie", is arrogant, rude, evasive or tends to exaggerate obviously.

6. *The effect of defendant's personal profile.* Add or subtract a separate 5% element to the settlement value sub-total if the defendant projects a strongly negative or positive personal image.

REMEMBER: Adding percentage points based upon these intangible case circumstances means that they favor the plaintiff, while subtracting points means the circumstances favor the defendant.

CASE EXAMPLE: USING THE "FSV" FORMULA

There is an actual case that demonstrates how to find a sensible settlement goal. Here is a summary of facts in a motor vehicle intersection accident case in which the claimant sustained a "whiplash" injury to neck and shoulder.

Issue Facts

—Claimant, McGraw, driving east on a through road. Defendant, Jones, driving north on an intersecting road with a stop sign at the corner facing him.

—McGraw and passenger, Weinen, claim their car going 50-55 m.p.h. in 60 m.p.h. zone and that Jones car entered intersection without stopping.

—Jones and passenger, Aram, say they stopped for the sign, then started into the intersection and saw claimant car 300-400 feet away and approaching. They claim McGraw was speeding, approximately 70-80 m.p.h.

—Disinterested witness, LaValle, driving car behind Jones, says latter slowed "almost but not quite to a stop," then started into the intersection under acceleration. At this time he saw claimant car approximately 100 feet away, approaching at a "normal" speed.

—Severe impact between front of claimant car and driver's side of Jones car.

—Claimant had immediate pain in neck and right shoulder. . .taken to hospital by ambulance. . .given emergency room treatment, x-rayed and released to own doctor, Dr. Bellows.

—Referred by lawyer to orthopedic specialist, Dr. Colon, who diagnosed injury as "cervical muscular and ligamentous sprain, non-permanent, with decreasing tenderness and disability for 6 months to 1 year."

—Expenses and losses to date: $35 hospital bill; $125 Dr. Bellows (6 visits & massage treatments over 10 months); $150 Dr. Colon (3 visits and 2 therapy sessions); $525 gross loss of wages (2 weeks).

Liability Issues And Comparative Evidence

	CLAIMANT	DEFENDANT
1. Defendant's negligence		
Witnesses:	McGraw, Weinen, LaValle	Jones, Aram
Testimony:	Defendant didn't stop at stop sign.	Did stop at sign
2. Proximate cause of Defendant's negligence		
Witnesses:	same	same
Testimony:	Defendant drove into intersection in front of claimant	Defendant drove into intersection in front of claimant
3. Contributory negligence of claimant		
Witnesses:	same	same
Testimony:	claimant driving 50-55 in 60 m/p/h zone	claimant speeding 70-80 in 60 m/p/h zone
4. Proximate cause of contributory negligence		
Witnesses:	same	same
Testimony:	claimant car struck defendant car in intersection	claimant car struck defendant car in intersection

Damage Issue And Comparative Evidence

1. **Claimant injury proximately resulting from collision**

Witnesses:	McGraw, Dr. Colon	none now
Testimony:	immediate pain neck & shoulder, continuing 6 weeks, then decreasing to slight pain on motion today . . . cervical muscle & ligament sprain	none now

Non-Issue Facts

The following information was gathered by claimant's counsel from a variety of sources, including defendant's statement, phone calls to two experienced trial lawyers and the Clerk of the local court, phone call to Dr. Colon and reference to the Jury Verdict Handbook. He also reviewed past personal injury cases he handled.

—*The highest plaintiff verdict reported in this jurisdiction over past 5 years,* involving similar injuries and expenses, was $3,750.

—*Defendant Jones, was covered by a liability policy* having single limits of $25,000.

—*It will cost claimant* an estimated $600 to sue through trial ($300 additional attorney fees based on a $2,000 verdict because of a fee increase from 25 to 40%; $150 trial fee for Dr. Colon and $150 deposition and transcript expense).

—*It will cost defendant (insurer)* an estimated $1,900 to defend a suit through trial ($1,500 attorney fees assuming a 3 day trial; $250 doctor fee for exam and testimony and $150 for depositions and transcripts).

—*There is no significant difference in skill and experience between attorneys.* (the lawyers who represents this insurance company is known).

—*The claimant has a pressing need for money.* He is a wage earner with no savings and bills to pay. (−5%)

—*Defendant is not a "target"* and has no personal financial exposure since he is adequately covered by insurance.

—*Claimant has a poor personality profile,* being poorly educated and somewhat belligerent in manner. (−5%)

—*Defendant has an average profile* with no apparent sympathy or antagonism potential.

Applying The Formula To The Case Facts

PAV —The verdict range is from a low of $835 (total of liquidated damages) to a high of $3,750. The average is $2,300.

%PPV—Neither side will be entitled to a direct verdict because in view of the witness disputes, liability issues must be resolved by the trier of facts, the jury. However, claimant had the right of way subject only to a finding that he was driving at an unlawful rate of speed. This advantage of law, coupled with favorable testimony of disinterested witness. LaValle, indicates a verdict for claimant is *clearly probable*. Estimate the percentage at 75%.

UV —none
PC —$600
DC —$1,900
I   —minus 10% (claimant's need and poor personality)

Working The Equation

$$(\$2,300 \times 70\% - \$600 + \$1,900) - 10\% = FSV$$
$$(\$1,610 + \$1,300 = \$2,910) - \$291 = \$2,619$$

Rounding off, the Fair Settlement Value is $2,600.

This value represents a settlement figure that is reasonable to both sides; it discounts their respective risks without excess, and it credits their potentials within limits. Claimant's maximum risk is a defendant's verdict (slight risk) and $300 non-contingent expenses. Defendant's maximum risk is a plaintiff's verdict in excess of $3,750 (moderate risk) and $1,900 non-contingent expenses.

How FSV Calculation Avoids Impulsive Evaluation

There is neither magic nor infallibility claimed for formula approaches to settlement values. With a procedure involving such diverse and slippery factors—a decision by twelve persons whose identities and prejudices are unknown to you—any attempt to guarantee a forecast is bound to be fradulently given and skeptically received.

Applying these techniques, then avoids the worst habit of lawyers in negotiation, the impulsive evaluation. It forces you to analyze and weigh your case strengths and weaknesses, assess future risks and expenses, and study past jury results. All for the purpose that is accomplished. . .to arrive at a reasoned rather than a sensed settlement goal.

> **REMEMBER: Fair Settlement Value is a guide, not a goal. It is a figure that is reasonable, not a settlement figure that is best. It is possible for you to do better than FSV as an advocate for either party—using negotiating techniques.**

KEY TECHNIQUES FOR PERSUASIVE BARGAINING

Negotiation has been characterized as modern man's substitute for the mace and broadsword. It isn't that force is missing altogether but that it is threatened rather than used, felt rather than seen.

This is a clue to successful settlement negotiation: The greater the force that one party believes the other party commands—whether he really commands it or not—the more willing the former will be to accept the latter's terms.

But force is not the only unseen presence having an impact on negotiations. Advantage is another. The greater the advantage to himself that one party *believes* he sees in his opponent's settlement proposal—as an alternative to trial—the more willing he is to accept it.

A trial is the equivalent of a military battle in this respect. In both, the appearance of force and advantage is of minor importance, for the imminent outcome measures their reality. At a pre-trial negotiation session, on the other hand, appearance is a big part of everything. If your opponent believes your liability evidence is strong and your law authoratative, isn't that as good as if they really are? If you convince plaintiff's counsel that your settlement terms net him more than a verdict will, isn't that as good as a low verdict itself? A lawyer-negotiator acts upon his beliefs; whether they are valid or not is immaterial to you whose techniques induced them.

How To Exploit Your Strengths—And Create Illusory Bargaining Power

The ability to exploit strengths and foster illusions at the bargaining table marks the repeatedly successful lawyer-negotiator. He wins a favorable settlement when his facts and law are strong by making them appear irresistible. But he also wins sometimes when his facts and law are weak by convincing his opponent they are not—without misrepresentation, of course.

He settles cases on his terms when they are advantageous to himself by making them appear advantageous to the other. And he also settles on terms obviously disadvantageous to the opponent by convincing the latter they are better than the results of a future trial.

The Six Functions Of Good Negotiating Techniques

Successful negotiating requires the use of techniques that fulfill the following six functions:

1. *Enable you to recognize your case strengths and your opponent's weaknesses.*
2. *Enable you to display those strengths and weaknesses in the most favorable light for your side.*
3. *Help you create the illusion of greater strength than you possess and greater weakness than he suffers from.*
4. *Help you create the illusion of more advantage to the opponent than your terms carry.*
5. *Enables you to induce in your opponent a confidence in your work and a respect for your ability.*
6. *Enables you to create a friendly atmosphere conducive to agreement.*

Here are some simple bargaining-room techniques you should always employ whatever side of a case you represent. They fulfill the functions listed previously. Moreover, no matter what your case or who your opponent, they will never be inappropriate to your goal, which is to settle on terms at least as good as and, hopefully, better than Fair Settlement Value.

HOW TO PROJECT AUTHORITY DURING NEGOTIATIONS

It is absolutely essential that you enter a negotiating session with a thorough knowledge of your case facts and law. Not just the favorable elements of both, but the unfavorable as well. Knowledge of the first enables you to recognize your case strengths and advance them with accuracy and authority. Knowledge of the second allows you to spot an error or exaggeration in the opponent's presentation and deflate his argument.

Knowledge is power, but it also conveys an authority that is irresistible. Know precisely what the witnesses will say and have their statements to support you. Know in depth what appellate courts and legislators say and have citations on hand. Know these things better than your opponent and see how quickly he is cowed—and how ready he is, grudgingly to be sure—to admit your expertize in other areas.

As rudimentary as this plea for knowledge sounds, it is the fate of many lawyers practising today to be bullied during negotiations. Time without number I have heard them begin talking money with only the foggiest notion of their case facts, and no notion at all about the law that applies. They open their files and all that is within is a copy of a police report or a contract or, perhaps, a half page, scribbled memo of what their clients told them. Other lawyers muster thick files filled with so many scraps and jots and jumbled records, in such disorder that it is impossible for them to find information they need. Nor, indeed, have they looked for it beforehand.

Case facts and law are not the only things you should know when you come to the bargaining table. Here is a list of all the essentials:

Checklist: Nine Items You Must Know Before You Bargain

1. *The Fair Settlement Value of your case.* Applying the "FSV" formula to your facts shortly before your first bargaining settlement. Wait as long as possible to compute the value so current facts may be considered. But don't start serious negotiation until you know a figure that represents the fair settlement level. Only by this means can you decide whether a settlement proposal your opponent makes is favorable or unfavorable to the client.

2. *If you represent claimant, know the minimum amount of money, property or performance your client has authorized you to accept in settlement.*

   If you represent defendant, know the maximum amount of money, property or performance the client has authorized you to pay in settlement.

   Discuss this minimum demand or maximum offer thoroughly with your client shortly before the negotiating session and obtain a firm and clear commitment. (Techniques for obtaining this commitment are discussed later in this chapter).

3. *Know the first demand you are going to make if you are for claimant or the first offer to that demand if you represent defendant.* Don't "play it by ear" as so many lawyers do, waiting to see how genial their opponent is or how much he offers before making their demand; or delaying a

decision on how much to offer until they see how firm the demand is and the opponent who makes it.

Decide beforehand what your first demand will be by fixing it at a level that is *reasonably excessive* relation to FSV if you represent plaintiff, or *reasonably deficient* if you represent defendant.

4. *Know your settlement objective;* i.e., in a claim for money damages, the least or largest amount of money you are willing to recommend the client accept or pay in settlement. If you represent claimant, this amount should be more than FSV and more than the client's minimum authorization. If you represent defendant, the sum should be less than his maximum authorization.

> REMEMBER: Your settlement objective will rarely remain fixed throughout the course of negotiations. It will rise or descend depending upon your opponent's reaction to your demand or offer and presentation, and your reaction to his. But settlement negotiation is like a journey by car; you should know where you want to go before you start.

5. *Know your case facts and evidence thoroughly.* Only if you have the facts can you defend and justify your demand or offer with specifics. Read the contents of your case file from cover to cover the day before the conference. Arrange your statements, memoranda, and documents in the order of your case issues (e.g., liability, then damages) for ready reference. If you represent claimant, total your liquidated damages after itemizing them, then group your supporting documents in the same order as the itemization (e.g., hospital and clinic bills, doctor bills, drug receipts, car repair estimates and bills, wage statements, and miscellaneous). Make copies of these documents and give a set to the adverse party, insurance representative or opposing counsel.

Note: adequate documentation of your liquidated damage claims improves the prospect of settlement, for it eliminates one form of challenge to them—that you exaggerate the total.

6. *Know the current law in your jurisdiction applying to the case issues.* Prepare an informal memorandum of case, statutory, and encyclopedia authorities for ready use during the settlement conference. List accurate citations following each stated authority.

An important element of persuasion is involved. Merely telling an opponent that, "California allows a loss of use recovery for the total destruction of a motor vehicle; I learned that during my research," is much less convincing than if you are able to say, "California allows a loss of use recovery. The Supreme Court said so in *Reynolds v Bank of America,* at 53 C. 2d 49."

7. *Know past verdicts in similar cases within your jurisdiction.* You will have already obtained this information for your FSV calculation. Select from the entire list those verdicts that favor your side (high verdicts if you represent claimant; low or defense verdicts if you represent defendant). Carry this selection into the conference and use it to support your demand or offer.

8. *Know the financial responsibility of the defendant.* If you represent claimant, know defendant's insurance coverages and policy limits (Techniques for uncovering insurance information before suit are presented in Chapter 8.) If there is coverage with high limits, mention it during the conference so the insurance representative or opposing counsel knows you know about it.

   If you represent an insured defendant with limits below FSV, mention the limits to your opponent. They will have a depressive effect on his demand and settlement objective.

   Finally, if defendant is not insured, know the nature and extent of his assets from your investigation into them (See Section A, Chapter 8 for techniques to determine financial responsibility). If his net assets exceed FSV, disclose your knowledge to defendant or his counsel (if he is represented). If you are defense counsel and his net assets are less than FSV, point the fact out to your opponent during the conference as support for your offer.

9. *When you represent claimant, know your opponent at the bargaining table. If the opponent is an unrepresented defendant,* know his employment, position, and salary or wages; know the character of his residential neighborhood (upper, middle or lower social class), and his credit standing. This information provides clues to incentives he has to avoid a lawsuit and possible judgment.

   If the opponent is an insurance representative, know his company's reputation for being quick, average or reluctant settlers; for making liberal, average, or stingy offers; for being willing or unwilling to increase an offer substantially, moderately, or only slightly. Know whether the representative has general authority to settle in the area of your settlement objective, only limited authority or perhaps none. You can learn this information from other local lawyers who have dealt with the company previously.

   Note: A fertile source of facts about an insurance company is an adjuster for another company. Phone an adjuster you know for information. If you don't know any, call an adjuster for your own liability insurer. In the competitive market of today, you will find him anxious to please.

If your opponent at the settlement conference is defense counsel, know the above information and also know him, i.e., his settlement habits and trial ability. If you don't know these characteristics from personal experience, ask other lawyers in your area about them. Seek answers to these questions:

—*Is he an outstanding, average or poor trial lawyer?*
—*What percentage of the cases does he settle; a high, average or low percentage? (If his trial ability is average or poor, a high settlement history probably means he recognizes his shortcomings and makes liberal offers.)*
—*Does he usually settle at the first conference, or only after repeated and prolonged haggling? (If the former, you can afford to reduce your demand more quickly toward the settlement objective. If the latter, you dare not do it more than gradually or you risk reaching the objective before he is willing to settle.)*
—*Does he have a busy practice? If he does, he has an added incentive to settle your case, for he knows his income increases as his case turnover does.*

WHEN YOU REPRESENT DEFENDANT: You need answers to the same questions about your opposing counsel as he does about you. If you don't know the answers yourself, seek them from other local lawyers who do. It has been my experience that lawyers are as ready to talk about other lawyers as wives are about other wives.

TO BE COMPELLING, BE CONFIDENT

Successful negotiating techniques perform a variety of functions that may be roughly grouped under two headings; fact disclosure and persuasion. Of the two, persuasion is the more important and the more difficult.

A settlement on your terms comes about because your opponent (defendant, insurance representative or other counsel) *believes* that it represents a better result than is likely at trial. And it makes no difference as far as the settlement is concerned whether the belief is based on fact or illusion.

Turning the proposition around, it makes no difference whether your evidence or law really is stronger than his, you will not settle at or near your terms unless you convince him that it is. If your bargaining technique is persuasive, you *can* convince him, not only when the strength is there but occasionally when it is not.

How Salesmanship Must Be Used In Bargaining

Persuasive bargaining technique involves substance, manifested in your knowledge of all factors favorably affecting settlement. It also involves form, manifested in your manner, exuding complete confidence in yourself and your case. It is a key lesson in salesmanship that you rarely succeed in selling a product unless you appear to be sold yourself, so you will have trouble selling your settlement terms, just as a salesman has trouble selling his vacuum cleaners, if the opponent-customer doubts your faith in your case, your proposal, or yourself.

> **ACTION RULE:** From the moment you begin negotiations until you end them, display perfect confidence in the merit of your case, your client, your witnesses, your settlement terms and yourself. By word and manner project to your opponent total assurance that should the case be tried, the resulting judgment will be worse for him than your demand or offer.

Checklist Of Techniques For Projecting Confidence

—*Use positive language in describing your evidence, law, witnesses, client, and his claims or defenses.* Pattern your language after these examples:

    —Say *"this evidence proves. . ."* not *"in my opinion, the evidence proves"*, or *"the evidence seems to prove"*.

    —Say *"these case authorities clearly support me . . ."* not *"according to my interpretation of these cases, they support me"*.

    —Say *„there's no doubt my client was injured, and that's what the jury will find"*, not *"I think I can prove he was injured"*.

    —Say *"I'll have no trouble proving your client was the aggressor in this marriage"*, not *"there's a question about who the aggressor was, but I think I can prove . . ."*

—*Emphasize and exaggerate a case strength; disparage and discount a case weakness.* Showing confidence does not mean being arrogant about your obvious strengths nor blind to visible weaknesses. But it does mean you should claim the greatest impact for the first and least effect—or none at all—for the second. Emphasize the strengths in some such fashion as in these examples:

> *My witness saw your client drive past the stop sign. That's negligence as a matter of law. And that means if I have to file suit, the only question for the jury will be how much money should the plaintiff get.*
>
> *He's a disinterested witness, with no axe to grind; he's bright, likeable, and he's mine. The jury's going to find a contract in this case because he was there when it was discussed and they'll believe him.*

Disparage and discount your weaknesses by explaining how little significance they possess, alone or when contrasted with the strengths . . . as in this example:

> *It's true my client was exceeding the prima facie speed limit. But that's not important for two reasons; first, the traffic was light, it was daytime, the road was dry and he was only 5 m.p.h. over. No judge or jury is going to find that speed unlawful. Second, even if he was going too fast, your man's the sole proximate cause of the accident. He crashed the stop sign and entered the intersection when my client was only 50 feet away. The collision would have happened even had my client been going 20 m.p.h.*

—*Always describe your settlement demand or offer as the best your opponent can expect under the case circumstances.* Say you are sure that if he will consider it in the light of your strong and his weak points, he will accept. Then summarize the points for him to be sure he overlooks none. *Never suggest you can lower a demand or increase an offer—even if you mean to—until you have used every persuasive technique to gain a settlement at the original level and it is positively rejected.*

> NOTE: Even after your opponent has positively rejected your settlement terms, do not modify them at the same conference at which they were announced. Wait some time for two reasons: he may change his mind (or his client for him) during the interim, and your credibility is hurt if you retreat from your terms quickly.

—*State your prediction of the verdict (judgment) if the case is sued on and tried, in terms of the best the opponent can expect* (if you represent claimant, say "the least amount of money the jury is going to return is $ "; if you represent defendant, say "the most the jury will return is $).

Then summarize the facts on which your prediction is based—proof of damages, measure of damages, past jury verdicts, etc. Say there is only a "remote chance" that a judge or jury will do more for his client than your demand or offer will. Never say, "the verdict can go either way" even if you are sure it can. Never say, "you may be able to win" even if you are sure he would. If your opponent has any doubts about his case, your phrasing must enlarge them. And if he has no doubts, you must introduce them.

—*Be positive about your ability to prove your issues if the case if tried.* Never concede any difficulty producing necessary evidence. If a witness or document is missing and your opponent asks about him(it), do not admit the disappearance. Simply say, "I'll produce him when it's necessary." Say it with assurance no matter how dubious you are and the opponent will assume you really can produce him.

—*Keep an even countenance and disposition throughout negotiations and never show anger, disappointment, or a wound.* Even though your opponent surprises you with new and damaging facts or law, don't flinch. Affect indifference to it or, if you can, show him how your case strengths offset it.

—*Speak about your past settlements and trial victories when they support* your present settlement proposal. Say that you mention them not to appear boastful but merely to illustrate the reasonableness of your demand or offer by actual precedents. Introducing past successes this way accomplishes three things: 1. It demonstrates a solid basis for your outcome prediction; 2. It indicates your experience and ability, and 3. It avoids the impression of conceit that would otherwise be made.

Boastfulness in a lawyer is a vice, because it produces resentment in his opponent and makes any agreement more difficult. But modesty is no virtue if it suppresses information useful in gaining a good settlement.

HOW TO GAIN TRUST AND RESPECT
FROM YOUR OPPONENTS

Among the traits a lawyer brings with him to a bargaining table, none are more damaging—more ruinous—to the prospect of settlement than discourtesy and dishonesty. Yet both are frequently seen there, sometimes alone and sometimes in combination.

Some lawyers are discourteous to their opponents by nature, some by design and some by accident, without being aware they are. Whatever prompts it, only a pressing need to settle will usually induce the opponent to do so with one who insults him by his manner.

> **ACTION RULE:** All other settlement factors being equal, a lawyer will settle earlier with and give better terms to an opponent he likes than an opponent he dislikes. And no trait is more likeable in an opponent than genuine courtesy.

Here are some specifics you should adopt and others you should avoid in order to gain a more friendly response from opponents. Adapt your negotiating conduct accordingly and your settlement experiences will be pleasanter—not only in atmosphere, but in accomplishment as well.

Checklist Of Courtesies That Create The Right Rapport

1. *Attend the settlement conference on time and prepared for a meaningful discussion.* Making him wait for your arrival or being unprepared after you come wastes his time. Since time is money for a lawyer, you will have found the quickest means to displease him if you are late.
2. *Bring your client or requested documents to the conference if you previously agreed to do so.* He will probably have agreed to some request you made, and failing your part tells him you cannot be trusted.
3. *Devote whatever time is necessary for a full discussion of case and settlement proposals.* Don't get up from the bargaining table after fifteen minues and say, "I've an appointment. I'll get back to you later and we'll finish this another time." With some opponents, negotiations will be finished then and there. Having allotted an hour for the conference and prepared himself another hour beforehand, he will be loath to risk further time on so flighty an adversary.
4. *Listen attentively to his presentation and proposal. No matter how much you may disagree, note the points of controversy and let him finish without interruption.* It is exasperating to negotiate with a lawyer who treats a settlement conference like a ping pong match, retorting to every statement his opponent makes. Remember Bierce's definition of a "bore" as "a man who speaks when you want him to listen." Listening without interruption is no indication of agreement or approval, so it does not lose a controversy. It merely reinforces an attitude of friendly discussion.
5. *Make a settlement proposal of your own and be prepared to justify, argue, and defend it.* Never attend a conference merely to hear what the other side will demand or offer, without binding yourself to a commitment of any kind. If you do, you might as well leave negotiating your cases to others, for the message will circulate quickly among the local Bar that negotiating with you is a waste of time.
6. *Treat his arguments and settlement proposal with respect and appear to*

give them serious consideration no matter how much you may disagree. Don't scoff and say his argument is naive or his proposal is an insult. Say, instead, that his argument is "well-stated" but you "cannot agree with it for these reasons . . ." Say his settlement proposal is a "step in the right direction" but "it's not good enough, for these reasons . . ."

7. *Don't contradict his description of specific evidence or legal authorities unless you know he is wrong and can prove it* (by reference to the evidence itself or a document containing it, or by reference to a case, encyclopedia, or statute citation). Even then, don't contradict him abrasively by saying, "That's not what the witness said" or "The case doesn't stand for that principle at all."

Say, instead, "It's possible the witness said that, but I seem to recall it differently. Yes, see it here in his statement" . . . or . . . "Excuse me, but I got a different reading from that case. I wrote the syllabus down and here's what it says . . ."

NOTE: While you should be positive in advancing your case position, for maximum persuasion, you should be tactful in contradicting your opponent's position, for minimum resentment.

8. *Be warm to your opponent in ways that create a quick rapport.* Shake his hand on greeting and leave-taking. Smile rather than glower. Address him by name throughout, his Christian name, preferably, unless he is much older than you. Show you enjoy his company, and your manner will say, "You and I are going to agree eventually and until then, I'll like being with you."

REMEMBER: It is human nature to respond favorably to tendered good will. And a favorable response is precisely what you want from a settlement conference.

Why Honesty Is The Best Negotiating Policy

There is a small but significant minority of lawyers in every community who intentionally lie during negotiations in hope of achieving a settlement advantage. They misrepresent evidence, misquote witnesses, and misstate law to win a better settlement.

There is a larger group of lawyers who would never lie intentionally about any settlement factor, but who would. . .and do. . .lie unintentionally about one. These men are reckless about the truth rather than unconcerned with it. They quote witnesses, cite legal authority and make claims for evidence without really knowing what any of the three represent.

Lawyers in these two classes sometimes achieve settlement triumphs from this persuasion built on falsehood. But the triumphs are few and fleeting. For even in urban communities the word soon spreads that "John can't be trusted . . .watch out for him . . .he'll misrepresent his case".

ACTION EXAMPLE: HOW ONE MISSTATEMENT DAMAGED A SUCCESSFUL CAREER

It isn't just the chronic liar who is injured by the reputation he earns. The man who has erred just once can sometimes suffer a mistrust that impairs his settlement fortunes for years. Let me illustrate the risk with an actual case.

I know a lawyer—call him Bill—with a fine reputation for integrity and a successful personal injury practice—until a few years ago. He was representing a woman driver who was horribly injured in an early morning two-car crash on a lonely stretch of country road. The other driver was insured by a national liability insurer under a high-limit policy.

The drivers disputed liability. Bill's claimant said the other driver veered over the center line, striking her. The latter swore it was she who did the veering. Physical facts at the scene were inconclusive. Bill canvassed farm houses in the area of the crash and was told about an eyewitness, a man who had stopped at a nearby house after the crash to call police, who told the residents "the male driver came across the road and hit the female driver head on."

Bill obtained a complete description of the man and his car. A farmer in the area thought he knew who the witness was. It seemed to Bill that it was only a matter of days before the man was found and his statement taken. Based on this confidence Bill told the insurance supervisor with whom he was negotiating "I have an eyewitness who will positively put your man on the wrong side of the road an instant before the crash."

The insurance company had confidence in Bill and believed his statement. It was December of the year, annual reporting time in the industry and the company did not want this case sued; they wanted it settled so the large cash reserve previously placed on the case could be released. So it *was* settled, for $24,000.

There was just one condition the company insisted upon. Bill was to submit a signed copy of the witness' statement before the check would issue.

It was little enough in the company's mind, but more than Bill could fulfill. For three months he frantically searched. Finally, he had to admit his failure. After that, three things happened to him. The settlement was rescinded. The case was tried to a defense verdict. And, it is a matter of common knowledge within the local Bar, Bill has not settled a case since with any insurance company, big or small.

> **ACTION RULE:** Whenever you negotiate with an opponent, be certain of your facts before you state them, be clear about what the witnesses say before you quote them; always be accurate in your citations to, representations about, and quotes from legal authorities and never make a claim about your case unless it is true.

Since most lawyers are honest by purpose, your concern must be to avoid being dishonest by accident. Testing the things you say for accuracy before you say them will save a great many embarrassments. "The severest punishment of a liar is never to be believed."